D0048366

THE ROCK BIBLE

Library of Congress Cataloging in Publication Number: 2008924742

ISBN: 978-1-59474-269-9

Printed in China
Typeset in P22 Franklin Caslon
Designed by Bryn Ashburn
Illustrations by Jonathan Williams

Assembled, organized, edited, and manifested by Henry H. Owings
Original concept by Henry H. Owings and Brian Teasley

Distributed in North America by Chronicle Books
680 Second Street
San Francisco, CA 94107

10 9 8 7 6 5 4 3 2 1

Quirk Books
215 Church Street
Philadelphia, PA 19106
www.quirkbooks.com

UNHOLY SCRIPTURE
FOR FANS & BANDS

Contents

Preface

Although there is much knowledge and understanding—even mastery—of rock and roll, there is much that is still unknown of its origin. Whence did *The Rock Bible* come? This generally accepted script, commonly referred to as the hallowed "Chunklet Version," was culled from scribes and ciphers in its near apocryphal form. Although perfect in almost every aspect, it still has many holes. Just a glance at the lineage will reveal that it can be traced on a bloodline only as far back as the turn of the last century. However, it takes only a cursory glance at a used record bin at a local record store to see that rock's family tree is considerably older, wiser, and much more desperately in need of a bath than anybody could ever anticipate. When considering the rampant anachronism of rock—whether it be medieval, tribal, oriental, mystical, or a bizarrely Bohemian combination of all of these—rock scholars must assume that rock—as it is known today—can be proven only as old as a century. Yet its existence may be as old as the dawn of humanity. In fact, it is that primary assumption that has brought us

everything we currently know about the subject.

So how do we know what is known so far in *The Rock Bible*? It was written on musty walls in rock club bathrooms, tucked away in album liner notes, scrawled on the sides of road cases, and strewn over the floors of countless tour buses. *The Rock Bible*'s origins come from the youngest of the young to the most fossilized of fossilized bands. For years, rock scholars have worked diligently searching for rock's most puzzling questions. However, these scholars have never been known to be the sharpest bunch. In 1981, they believed that rock was invented in the 1960s and later perfected in the 1970s. It is from this very critical misunderstanding that the misnomer "classic rock" originated. In the '80s, there was a shift in the belief that perfection had been achieved, and scholars began to look toward the future for the answer. This led to a generation of music whose style and substance were as disposable as the musical equipment with which it was performed. It was soon discovered that all of their throw-away bleeps and bloops were just aching to be nothing more than the sum of their rock ancestors.

Finally, once the pot haze lifted, rock scholars backpedaled to say that rock was born when the southern United States* pulled their heads out of the red clay and discovered rock under a pile of burnt cinders left behind from an old-fashioned book burning. And from this, rock was born. It was not until very recently that scholars made a monumental breakthrough when ancient texts were unearthed that proved rock's age to be more than twice that originally believed and that there was even more to be discovered about its genealogy. These ancient texts were deciphered from a scratched-up 78 dredged from an abandoned farmhouse in Abingdon, Virginia. The artist, heretofore credited as Deaf Smokey Green, sang a song titled "That Rock, It Rolled," which was about a rock that he bought from a rich white guy. When Green thought he had been double-crossed, it turned out that this rock was the ancient key to playing the blues. He accidentally dropped it off a cliff, and chased after it, but it was forever lost. Finding this rock, and subsequently breaking its code, was critical in the interpretation of what you read here today. So you might be asking yourself where we found the rock. It was bought off an aging record collector in Maryland whose love of money is far greater than his actual love of the rock.

So as the broken beer bottles and cigarette butts are swept from rock's altar, let *The Rock Bible* live! As the throngs of rowdy concert-goers are herded out of the church, let it ring out! For those who heckled during communion, let it endure! And for those who asked for autographs, let it humbly exist. For those about to embark on their journey of reading this, *The Rock Bible* will last eternally.

HENRY H. OWINGS

---

*This is excluding Florida which, other than its geographic location, has never been Southern.

Introduction

The Bible. The epic window into which humans can see God. The celestial ascent into one supreme spiritual law. The inspired word of God set forth in the sole guide one needs for true divinity. THE ONE AND ONLY HOLY BOOK OF GOD OUR FREAKING LORD AND SAVIOR. I read such things as I scroll through literally hundreds of Bibles and books about the Bible at my local mega-mart bookstore. The Bible, it seems, far outnumbers any other book or movie franchise in sequels, spin-offs, and deleted scenes. If God intended to have only one sacred piece of work, then he sure didn't count on all the sub-par rip-off acts he would inspire.

Jesus . . . Effin' . . . Christ! Excuse me, but there are more than 3,000 translations of the Bible in English alone. Not to mention all the thousands of guidebooks that litter shelves like rat droppings. There are even hip, magazine-sized blurb Bibles for the pre- and just post-pubescent that read and look like very prudish versions of adult fashion magazines. Not only that, there are porn mags for Christians done by porn actors/actresses who have

waited until marriage to have sex with another porn actor/actress who has also waited until marriage to have sex with the aforementioned partner he or she just married. Okay, I just made that up, but maybe that's because I want to dream it to come true!

Anyway, as I peruse the aisles of planet corporate bookstore, I realize something: Who else seems to have a lot of Bibles besides these crazy Christians? Golfers. Golfers seem to love golf Bibles or Bibles with plaid-sweatered golf motifs. Actually, it seems that every two-bit hobby has a Bible . . . except for rock and roll. But why should we introduce a new Bible unto the already festering heap of unread thin-sheeted parables? Never before has the overwhelming majority of Christians been rivaled by another group. Until now! Now, there is a new demographic disease spreading like salmonella in a bowl of frat boy barf. That's right dear reader. . . . The group I refer to is you and your lousy band.

It is time we punished you for all your sins and sent you on the way of the enlightened. And why us?

Because it is the staff of Chunklet World Industries who has suffered through all your feeble attempts at noise-making. We have bore the brunt of your feeble first misfires; your butterfingered live show blundering, your soulless, sloppy-second sophomoric studio hijinks; your mopey, makeshift stylistic missteps; and, our favorite, your inevitable career-ending mistakes. Furthermore, we have fully notorized authority to write this book because, in full disclosure, most of us play in lousy bands ourselves, or at least load in the gear, tune the guitars, set the lights, promote the show, design the posters, sweep the floors, or count the money. Yours truly has clocked in for more than 2,500 shows with a wide variety of bands, and I have actually seen, smelt, and dealt every shade of horrible imaginable.

So stand on our shoulders, dear rocker—the shoulders of rock. You can view this book as an all-purpose guide to how not to be in a crappy band or translate the Bible of Rock into your otherwise rockless civilian life. No matter. What you hold before you will inevitably be outselling the Bible itself. Unlike fossil fuels or good band names, there is no foreseeable end to bad music. That is, unless you heed our divine word and follow this book as if it were a Bible—which it is. It is indeed *The Rock Bible*. And so what if we didn't die for your sins? What have you ever done for us?

BRIAN TEASLEY

A Little Rock Bible Essay

The embracing of rock and roll has become a lazy pastime for consumers and spectators. There's no sincerity in it. Rock is "funny" to those who are not funny, and rock is easy for those who don't know how to rock but need a career makeover. Every shitty fourth or fifth album by a once-decent band is the one that "goes back to the rock." Conversely, rock never died. Musicians who say that are just trying to over-intellectualize their own pretentious crap. And yet rock is in trouble, and some rules need to be adhered to. That's why this book is important.

When it takes someone like played-out and prosaic garbage Tenacious D to qualify as rock culture satire, you know that we live in the ultimate culture of creative bankruptcy. This level of rock commentary is designed to make thirty-something, Dockers-donning, borderline date rapists laugh while they say things like "lemme buy you a drink" at a wedding reception's free bar. Just look at the types of people who laugh at rock. Any asshole who's discovered rock music through the recordings of the Eagles of Death Metal just needs to go back to trading tit comments at the water cooler.

Rock has lost something and needs a set of rules. Sadly, in this day and age the only true way to rock is to commit suicide on stage. Given the current glut of awful rock bands, this proposed trend couldn't hurt. Regardless, there are ways to Rock-It-Up and non-rocking bad habits to alleviate. This book serves the veteran and the charlatan. Don't feel bad if you just discovered Thin Lizzy last year (but for God's sake, don't tell anyone). You can be helped. And for the old-ass windbags and retro-robots out there: This is the 21st century. Nothing that was made in the '50s or early '60s still rocks.

It is my hope that *The Rock Bible* finds its way into the glove compartments of all touring bands' vans and/or buses. I hope that it changes the face of music, thus creating more music that actually does rock.

ANDREW EARLES

N the beginning, Thomas Edison invented the phonograph, which begat the publishing of "Memphis Blues" by Hart Wand in 1912 (often credited as the first blues title), which begat W. C. Handy writing "St. Louis Blues" (often credited as the first real blues song) in 1914, which begat the Chicago Automatic Machine & Tool Company inventing the jukebox in 1915, which begat the bluesman Leadbelly being imprisoned for murder in 1917, which begat Buster Smith's move to Dallas, which begat "Blind" Lemon Jefferson recording "Long Lonesome Blues" for Paramount in Chicago in 1926, which begat "Blind" Lemon Jefferson becoming the first commercially successful bluesman, which begat the words "rock and roll" (which were black slang for sexual intercourse) appearing on record for the first time in Trixie Smith's "My Man Rocks Me with One Steady Roll" in 1922, which begat the introduction of the 78 RPM record in 1929, which begat the George Beauchamp invention of the electric guitar known as the Frying Pan in 1931, which begat the release of Count Basie's "One O'Clock Jump" in 1937, which begat John Hammond's staging of the "Spirituals to Swing" concert in New York City to highlight black musical styles in 1938, which begat Leo Mintz opening "The Record Rendezvous" a Cleveland, Ohio, store specializing in "race" music in 1939, which later begat the playing of those records by DJ Alan Freed, which launched the rock 'n' roll era, which begat the debut of Billboard Magazine's Harlem Hit Parade to chart the top singles in the "race" field, a precursor to rhythm & blues, in 1942, which begat the slowing growth of rhythm blues music due to the onset of World War II, resulting in limited record production until the war's end in 1945, which begat the opening in 1943 of King Records in Cincinnati, Ohio, to record hillbilly music, which begat the formation of Modern Records, one of the most successful and groundbreaking R&B labels in the country, by the Bihari family of Los Angeles in 1945, which begat the invention by people like Pierre Schaeffer and the engineers at Sun Records of echo-delay, a multitrack recording technique, which begat the formation of Imperial Records by Lew Chudd, which begat 1946's biggest hit ever ("Choo Choo Ch'Boogie") in the increasingly popular jump blues style, which begat the 1947 introduction by The Ravens of a new form of harmony singing featuring a bass vocalist floating on top of the melody, which begat the 1947 start of Atlantic Records by Ahmet Ertegun and Herb Abramson, which begat the term "rhythm & blues," coined by future Atlantic Records producer Jerry Wexler, which begat the #1 R&B hit by The Orioles "It's Too Soon to Know," the first rock ballad, which begat the June 1948 Columbia launch of the vinyl 12-inch 33 1/3 RPM album, which begat the saxophone becoming the centerpiece sound of R&B, which begat the electric guitar taking hold with the blues recordings of T-Bone Walker, John Lee Hooker, and Muddy Waters, which begat failing white Memphis radio station WDIA hiring Nat Williams, the first black DJ, and also the hiring of B.B. King and Rufus Thomas as DJs, which begat the March 31, 1949, introduction by RCA Victor of the smaller and cheaper 45 RPM record along with a small, inexpensive record player for $12.95, which begat the massive hit "Saturday Night Fish Fry," which marks the end of the jump blues dominance of the 1940s, which begat Jimmy Preston's raucous "Rock the Joint," pointing toward a new horizon of rock 'n' roll, which begat the 1950 release of Fats Domino's first record "The Fat Man," ushering in the full-fledged rock sound, which begat huge smashes and chart toppers by Little Esther, Mel Walker, The Robins, Ivory Joe Hunter, Percy Mayfield, and Laurie Tate, which begat the record "Hot Rod Race" by Arkie Shibley & His Mountain Dew Boys, which set the stage for white country music to meet R&B in a term to be known as "rockabilly," which begat Atlantic Record's first #1 record of the '50s, which was Ruth Brown's "Teardrops from My Eyes," which begat the 1951 wave of young black vocal groups The Five Keys, The Clovers, and The Dominoes, which begat the introduction of the first jukebox playing 45 RPM records, which begat Sam Phillips of Memphis recording Ike Turner's band performing "Rocket 88," which further cemented rock's future as raucous, exciting, and dangerous, which begat Les Paul's dazzling electric guitar work on the #1 hit "How High the Moon," which begat the June 1951 "Moondog Show," by Cleveland DJ Alan Freed on WJW, broadcasting nothing but R&B, which begat the 1952 recording of "Rock the Joint" by renegade white country-and-western swing band Bill Haley and the Saddlemen, which begat the white pop vocalist Johnny Ray's recording of the two-sided smash "Cry" b/w "The Little White Cloud That Cried," which begat the belief that Johnny Ray was both black and a woman, which begat the recording of massive hits by Johnny Ace, B. B. King, Bobby "Blue" Bland, Lloyd Price, Fats Domino, and Charles Brown, which begat the first hit "Hard Times" written by Jerry Leiber and Mike Stoller, which begat Sam Phillips starting his own label, Sun Records, in Memphis, with their first release being Johnny London's "Drivin' Slow," which begat on the night of March 21, 1952, DJ Alan Freed putting on the first ever rock 'n' roll show in Cleveland, which begat in 1953 Bill Haley changing his group's name to Bill Haley & the Comets and recording the first white rock hit, "Crazy Man Crazy," which begat the R&B charts beginning to reflect the overwhelming dominance of emerging rock 'n' roll, which begat the selling of 15 million R&B records bought in 1953, which began to draw attention in the industry but failed to note the growing interest among young white audiences that would soon have a major impact on society as a whole, which begat Ray Charles in 1954 forming his own band, which begat the R&B music explosion into the mainstream, which begat the pop record companies trying to capitalize on the perceived fad by having white artists cover black vocal-group records with increased distribution and radio play, assuring that many of those versions would become bigger hits, which begat widespread bans of such records as "Honey Love," "Such a Night," "Sexy Ways," and "Work with Me Annie," which begat the attendance of 10,000 fans at Alan Freed's first East Coast Rock 'n' Roll Show held in Newark, New Jersey, which was further proof that rock 'n' roll had national appeal, which begat Freed moving to New York's WINS and quickly becoming the city's most famous DJ, attracting massive audiences to his newly named "Rock 'n' Roll Party," which begat in Memphis Elvis Presley recording his first commercial hit "That's All Right, Mama" at Sun Studios, which begat the first tragedy of rock 'n' roll when its biggest star, Johnny Ace, accidentally shot and killed himself when playing Russian roulette backstage at a Houston auditorium between shows on

Christmas night, which begat in 1955 the Bill Haley and the Comets hit "Rock Around the Clock," from the film *Blackboard Jungle*, becoming the first rock record to top the pop charts for two months and remaining in the top 100 for a record 38 weeks, a record that would stand for 39 years, which begat Chuck Berry's "Maybellene" cracking the Top 5 on the pop charts and ushering in descending pentatonic double stops, which became the essence of rock guitar, which begat Bo Diddley's self-titled debut record topping the R&B charts and introducing the tribal "Bo Diddley" beat to rock, which begat radio blackballing of The Midnighters, which begat a May 1955 rock 'n' roll show by Fats Domino in Connecticut being cancelled for fear it would lead to rioting, which begat the banning of all further rock concerts in the state, which begat Boston following suit and banning dirty rock records from being played on the air, which begat the prevalence of censorship, with Pat Boone having the biggest impact with his watered-down versions of R&B hits, which begat Elvis Presley's contract being bought by RCA for the unheard of price of $35,000, which begat *Encyclopedia Britannica*'s referring to rock music as "jungle music," which begat in 1956 Elvis Presley's appearance in his national television debut on *The Dorsey Brothers Stage Show* in late January and a month later his first RCA record, "Heartbreak Hotel," racing up the charts neck and neck with his former Sun Records cohort Carl Perkins's "Blue Suede Shoes" as they claimed the #1 and #2 spots, which begat Presley scoring five #1 hits in a seven-month span, causing a sensation with his explosive performance of "Hound Dog" on *The Milton Berle Show*, appearing twice on *The Ed Sullivan Show* in the fall to enormous ratings, and releasing his first film in November, which begat rock 'n' roll entering the movies with cheaply made "rocksploitation" films by rockers singing their latest hits, the biggest and best of which was *The Girl Can't Help It*, starring Jayne Mansfield and featuring performances by Little Richard, Fats Domino, and Eddie Cochran, which begat the invention of feedback by The Johnny Burnette Rock 'n' Roll Trio on their record "The Train Kept A-Rollin," which begat the conviction of Gene Vincent for public obscenity with a fine of $10,000 by the state of Virginia for singing the erotic "Woman Love" onstage, which begat "I Put a Spell on You" by Screamin' Jay Hawkins selling more than one million records but facing a complete radio ban due to its "cannibalistic nature," thus becoming rock's first underground hit, which begat Elvis Presley's final *Ed Sullivan* appearance being filmed from the waist up, which begat the filming of *Jailhouse Rock*, considered the best rock film, starring Elvis Presley and introducing a precursor to the rock video, with the title song's elaborate jail-cell setting choreographed by Presley himself, which begat Bill Haley & the Comets' European tour setting off riots and bringing rock 'n' roll to that continent for the first time, which begat an Australian tour featuring Jerry Lee Lewis and Buddy Holly making rock a worldwide phenomenon, which begat Lewis's performance of "Whole Lotta Shakin' Goin' On" on *The Steve Allen Show*, bringing rock music more reprimands as Lewis kicked over his piano stool and played the keyboards with disturbing, wild-eyed intensity, which begat the stroll becoming the first dance associated with rock, which begat the cancellation of Alan Freed's short-lived televised rock 'n' roll show when complaints poured in over black teenage singer Frankie Lymon dancing on screen with a white girl, which begat society's first move to tame rock 'n' roll with the launch of ABC television's *American Bandstand*, which begat the Everly Brothers hit "Wake Up Little Susie" being banned from the airwaves due to lyrical content, which begat Little Richard, while on a tour in Australia, seeing the Russian satellite Sputnik descending to earth and taking it as a sign from God to quit rock 'n' roll and join the ministry, which begat in 1958 the induction of Elvis Presley into the U.S. Army for a two-year hitch overseas, which begat Ricky Nelson's "Poor Little Fool," boasting his first #1 record, which begat Alan Freed being indicted by Boston authorities for inciting a riot at a rock 'n' roll show he promoted because the audience stormed the stage during both Jerry Lee Lewis's and Chuck Berry's closing sets, which begat Jerry Lee Lewis's first British tour ending in scandal when people learned his third wife was his 13-year-old second cousin, forcing Lewis to cut the tour short and getting him blackballed by American radio and television upon his return to the United States, which begat the hits "Summertime Blues," "Sweet Little Sixteen," and "Yakety

Yak," all focusing on teenagers' struggles with parents, which begat Chuck Willis's double-sided, posthumous hit "What Am I Living For/Hang Up My Rock 'n' Roll Shoes" being the first rock record released in stereo engineered by Tom Dowd of Atlantic Records, which begat the power chord first appearing in records by guitarists Link Wray and Eddie Cochran, which begat distortion for electric guitar being first used by Lowman Pauling and a primitive form of fuzz bass being found on some records, which begat "Hard-Headed Woman" by Elvis Presley becoming the first rock record to "go gold," which begat the deaths in 1959 of Buddy Holly, Ritchie Valens, and the Big Bopper in a plane crash while on tour in Clearlake, Iowa, on February 3, which begat that date becoming known as "The Day the Music Died," which begat the National Academy of Recording Arts and Sciences sponsoring the first Grammy Awards ceremony for music, which begat Frank Sinatra winning his first Grammy award, which begat Congress opening the payola hearings designed to squash rock 'n' roll DJs who received money from record distributors in exchange for airplay, a common practice in all forms of radio for years, with Alan Freed, its main target and biggest casualty, being found guilty and taken off the air, which begat radio stations responding by voluntarily putting severe restrictions on what they would play, including a widely adopted Top 40 format that limited how many songs were approved for airing, which begat Dick Clark distancing himself from rock 'n' roll's bad image as he increasingly showcased the untalented "teen idols" on *American Bandstand*, which begat the rock instrumental having its biggest year ever in response to rock music facing bans for lyrical content, which begat Ray Charles bursting into the mainstream after years as an R&B star with "What'd I Say," which begat a new version of The Drifters using strings and introducing Latin rhythms to rock with the hit "There Goes My Baby," which begat the start of Tamia-Motown Records by Berry Gordy, which eventually became the most successful black-owned and black-operated company in American history with 600 million records sold, which begat the market share for rock 'n' roll increasing from 15.7 to 42.7 percent, making it the fastest-growing style of music ever, which begat John Coltrane forming his own quartet in 1960 and becoming the voice of jazz's New Wave movement, which begat Elvis Presley's appearance on *The Ed Sullivan Show* after his service in the army, which begat in 1961 big soul hits for groups like The Shirelles, The Marvelettes, and Dion, splitting from the Belmonts, which begat Patsy Cline releasing "I Fall to Pieces" and "Crazy," which helped her cross over from country to pop, which begat in 1962 the release of The Supremes' first record by Motown and the twist taking off, which begat Surf music ruling the airwaves in 1963, which begat The Beatles hitting America in 1964, leading the British invasion, which begat Bob Dylan plugging in at the Newport Folk Festival in 1965, spawning folk rock, which begat The Monkees' television series in 1966, which begat The Beach Boys' *Pet Sounds* album, which begat the beginning of the Monterey Pop Festival in 1967, which begat the open-air rock festival concept, which begat the release of *Sgt. Pepper's Lonely Hearts Club Band* by The Beatles, which begat Cream issuing their first two albums, which begat The Velvet Underground hooking up with Andy Warhol, which begat the MC5

playing the Grande Ballroom on October 30/31, 1968, and recording "Kick Out the Jams," which begat Elektra signing The Stooges after a record exec saw them opening for the MC5, which begat the Frank Zappa and the Mothers of Invention release of "We're Only in It for the Money" in 1968, which begat the 1969 Woodstock Music & Arts Festival drawing one half million fans to Max Yasgur's Farm in New York and the introduction of The Who's rock opera *Tommy*, which begat the 1970 fusion of jazz with rock to form jazz-rock or fusion, which begat the 1970 deaths of Jimi Hendrix and Janis Joplin from drug overdoses within one month of each other, which begat the release of The Grateful Dead's *Workingman's Dead and American Beauty* and the breakup of The Beatles, which begat the 1971 deaths of Jim Morrison (The Doors) and Duane Allman (Allman Bros. Band) and the release of songwriter Carole King's *Tapestry*, which begat Smokey Robinson leaving The Miracles to go solo in 1972, which begat the 1973 record-breaking tour of Led Zeppelin and Pink Floyd's release of *Dark Side of the Moon*, which begat the Jamaican film *The Harder They Come* starring Jimmy Cliff launching the popularity of reggae music in the U.S., which begat the 1974 tour of Bob Dylan and The Band and the release of Patti Smith's "Hey Joe," which is considered to be the first punk-rock single, which begat Cleveland's Rocket from the Tombs splitting into Pere Ubu and the Dead Boys, which begat The New York Dolls imploding in 1975 in Florida while on tour and their manager Malcolm McLaren fleeing back to London to try to re-create a more manageable version of the band later by way of The Sex Pistols, which begat in 1975 Television recording a demo tape with Brian Eno for Island Records, who then decided not to sign the band, which begat Richard Hell leaving the band to form The Heartbreakers with former New York Dolls guitarist Johnny Thunders, which begat The Sex Pistols playing their first gig at St. Martin's College, opening for Bazooka Joe, whose lead singer, Stuart Goddard, soon changed his name to Adam Ant and formed his own punk band called Adam and the Ants, which begat Rod Stewart officially quitting The Faces and Bruce Springsteen releasing "Born to Run," which begat Stevie Wonder's 1976 release of *Songs in the Key of Life*, which would win five Grammy awards, and the release of *Frampton Comes Alive*, which begat The Ramones making their first non-U.S. appearance supporting the Flamin' Groovies at the Roundhouse, which begat the UK punk scene, which begat Malcolm McLaren organizing a two-day punk festival at the 100 Club on Oxford Street in London with performers Subway Sect, Siouxsie and the Banshees, The Clash, The Sex Pistols, Stinky Toys, Chris Spedding, The Vibrators, The Damned, and The Buzzcocks, which begat the punk fanzine publication of *Sniffin' Glue*, which begat Mark Perry forming the band Alternative TV, which begat the releases of The Damned, The Saints, and The Sex Pistols' first singles, "New Rose," "(I'm) Stranded," and "Anarchy in the UK," respectively, which begat the Anarchy Tour with The Sex Pistols, The Damned, and The Clash, which begat the appearance of The Sex Pistols and several members of the Bromley Contingent, including Siouxsie Sioux and Steve Severin live on ITV to be interviewed by TV host William Grundy at which the band unleashed a torrent of curse words, which begat the following day's headline in the *Daily Mirror*, "The Filth and the Fury," which begat the 1977 disco influence being felt as *Saturday Night Fever* became a best-selling album, which begat the release of Meatloaf's *Bat Out of Hell*, which begat The Sex Pistols' release of *God Save the Queen*, which reached #2 on the British charts before it was banned by BBC Radio 1 and the title was left blank in the chart listings, which begat the opening of The Roxy Club in London at which The Clash played, which begat the firing of bassist Glen Matlock from The Sex Pistols, which begat his replacement being Sid Vicious, which begat Matlock forming The Rich Kids, which begat The Stranglers embarking on a 3-month nationwide tour, which begat The Sex Pistols renting a boat to take them down the Thames River during Queen Elizabeth II's Silver Jubilee anniversary celebration, where the police forced the boat to dock and several Pistol fans were injured in the melee and arrested, including Pistols manager Malcolm McLaren, Vivienne Westwood, and Bromley Contingent members Tracie O'Keefe and Debbie Juvenile, which begat Roxy Club DJ Don Letts filming *The Punk Rock Movie*, which begat the release of The Sex Pistols album *Never Mind the Bollocks, Here's the Sex Pistols*, which reached #1 on the British charts (despite being banned by most of Britain's record shops), which begat the October 20 plane crash killing 4 members of Lynyrd Skynyrd, which begat the 1977 death of Elvis Presley at age 42, which begat the 1978 introduction of the Sony Walkman, the first portable stereo, which begat Van Halen releasing their first album in 1978, which begat SST Records being formed by the Black Flag guitarist/founder Greg Ginn, which begat the end of The Sex Pistols's disastrous U.S. tour, during which Johnny Rotten walked off the stage at their Winterland concert in San Francisco, famously uttering, "Ever get the feeling you've been cheated?" which begat Sex Pistols bassist Sid Vicious being charged with murder in connection with the stabbing death of his girlfriend Nancy Spungen, who was found dead at New York's Chelsea Hotel, which begat the Rough Trade Records music store becoming a record label signing almost exclusively punk-inspired bands, which begat film director Derek Jarman releasing the cult punk-themed film *Jubilee* featuring Adam Ant, Toyah Willcox,

Siouxsie and the Banshees, and Malcolm McLaren protégé and early punk fashionista Jordan, which begat Blondie achieving worldwide success with their third album *Parallel Lines*, mixing together the style of '60s vocal pop, garage, and the energy of the new punk rock movement, which begat Debbie Harry becoming a new icon for the younger generations, which begat the death of Sex Pistols's Sid Vicious from a heroin overdose at the age of 21, which begat the 1979 release of two movies by The Who, who go on tour and 11 fans are trampled to death at their Cincinnati concert, which begat the invention by Phillips of the audio CD, which begat the Tesco Vee fanzine *Touch and Go*, which would be a highly influential label, which begat the 1980 murder of John Lennon in front of his New York apartment, which begat Joy Division lead singer Ian Curtis committing suicide at the age of 23, which begat creation of Dischord records in Washington, D.C., which begat the rest of the band going on to become New Order, which begat The Germs' lead singer Darby Crash committing suicide at the age of 22, which begat KROQ establishing the Top 106.7 Countdown, which The Clash and

Dead Kennedys both reached the same year, which begat documentary filmmaker Penelope Spheeris capturing the Los Angeles punk scene in the cult hit *The Decline of Western Civilization*, featuring interviews by Southern California punk bands Alice Bag Band, Black Flag, Catholic Discipline, Circle Jerks, Fear, The Germs, and X, which begat the release of the semidocumentary film *Rude Boy* starring Ray Gange as a roadie for The Clash, which begat R.E.M. debuting their singular brand of Soouthern-infused jangle rock at St. Mary's church in Athens, Georgia, which begat Henry Rollins becoming lead singer of Black Flag, which begat the disbanding in 1981 of Paul McCartney's Wings after 20 hits, which begat the debut of MTV running around-the-clock music videos, debuting with "Video Killed the Radio Star" by the Buggles, which begat critic Lester Bangs OD'ing on cold medicine in 1982, which begat the 1982 disbanding of The Eagles until Hell froze over, which begat members of Crass, The Mob, The Apostles, and others squatting the Zig Zag Club in west London and putting on a free all-day event featuring a number of anarcho-punk bands, which begat the release of Michael Jackson's

"Thriller," which begat the creation of Sludge rock powerhouse The Melvins, which begat the 1982 release of David Bowie's #1 hit "Let's Dance" with Stevie Ray Vaughn on guitar, which begat the debut of the Oklahoma Acid rock spectacle known as the Flaming Lips, which begat the 1984 death of Jackie Wilson, which begat the 1985 recording of "We Are the World" by 46 artists in support of suffering people in the USA and Africa, which begat the death of D. Boon of Minutemen in a car accident later that year, which begat the 1986 Lifetime Achievement Grammy being awarded to The Rolling Stones, which begat the Minneapolis-based record label Amphetamine Reptile bringing a scary, yet vibrant new sound to the table, which begat the 1987 tour of Russia by Billy Joel, which begat Whitney Houston earning her 7th consecutive #1 single in 1988, which begat CDs outselling vinyl records for the first time, which begat superstar ensemble The Traveling Wilburys release of an album just before Roy Orbison died, which begat Milli Vanilli's win of Best New Artist Grammy in 1989 only to have the award revoked when it was revealed they did not sing on their own debut album, which begat the emergence of two dominant '90s record labels Merge and Matador, which begat the unquestionably great band The Jesus Lizard, which begat the emergence in 1990 of hip-hop and a Hard Bop revival, which begat Curtis Mayfield (The Impressions) being paralyzed preparing for a stage concert and Stevie Ray Vaughn being killed in a helicopter crash in 1990, which begat Cardinal O'Connor asking the Pope to excommunicate Madonna and the release of Guns N' Roses *Use Your Illusion I and II* in 1991, which begat the death of Queen's Freddie Mercury from complications related to AIDS, which begat Perry Farrell's outdoor arena-filling spectacle of Lollapalooza, which begat Seattle becoming the core of grunge rock with groups like Nirvana and Pearl Jam and Prince changing his name in 1992, which begat the end of U2's 2-year Zoo/Zooropa World Tour in 1992, which begat compact discs surpassing cassette tapes as the preferred medium for recorded music, which begat the creation of *Chunklet*, the world's most influential magazine, which begat the not-as-influential rock magazine *Magnet*, which begat inception of the Omaha-based Saddle Creek label, which begat the 1994 suicide of Kurt Cobain, which begat the beginning of a new British Rock

Invasion by bands like Blur, Oasis, and Pulp, which begat the opening of the Rock and Roll Hall of Fame Museum in Cleveland, which begat the Washington State all-girl power troupe Sleater-Kinney, which begat Neil Young and Pearl Jam recording and performing together, which begat the formation of alt-country experimentalist Wilco, which begat the teaming up of Mariah Carey and Boys II Men for "One Sweet Day," which topped the charts in 1996 for an unprecedented 16 consecutive weeks, which begat Janet Jackson becoming the highest-paid musician in history when she signed an $80 million deal with Virgin Records, which begat every indie band that got signed to a major label during the Nirvana craze being dropped, which begat the 1997 Lilith Tour spotlighting female headliners, which begat the debut of ex-Kyuss members new band The Queens of the Stone Age and the emergence of red-and-white-clad duo The White Stripes, which begat the snuggly soft sounds of the Glaswegian band Belle and Sebastian, which begat the formation of Sub Pop tunesmiths The Shins and Bellingham-based good-intention rockers Death Cab for Cutie, which begat the 1998 death of Frank Sinatra at the age of 82 and the exit of Ginger Spice from the popular Spice Girls and The Rolling Stones giving concerts in Russia and Ringo Starr's Fourth All Starr Band, which begat the 1999 release of Anson Funderburgh & The Rockets featuring Sam Myers chart #1 on Living Blues radio poll, which begat the merger of two major recording labels, Universal and Polygram, causing upheaval in the recording industry, which begat the kick-off of Woodstock '99 in Rome, New York, which begat concertgoers complaining that the spirit of the original Woodstock had been compromised and commercialized, which begat trust-fund brats The Strokes temporarily taking over everything in music, which begat the sad murder (some claim "suicide") of Elliot Smith in his home in Los Angeles, which begat arty disheveled Canadian collective The Arcade Fire swaying dominance over the world of smarmy record store employees worldwide, which begat the Dead rising and every band that had ever been together reuniting for one last reunion tour, well maybe not "the" last.

BRIAN TEASLEY

O N the first day, God created the drums and cymbals. Now the drums were without rhythm and tempo, beatlessness reigned, and the Spirit of Rock hovered over the stage. In the future (and God knew this), beatlessness would become a needless sub-sub-sub-genre of the needless genre of "free jazz." Though God made very few mistakes in the creation of rock, allowing free jazz to slip through was one of them.

And God said, "Let there be drums," and there were drums. God saw that the drums were loud, and he separated the drums from the cymbals. God called the drums "rhythm," and the cymbals he called "kind of annoying." And there was a beat, and there was a solo, and solos would provide other members of the band the needed time to have sex with groupies, because God knew that no one would want to have sex with the drummer.

The Psalm of the Drummer

1 The reason there are so many drummer jokes is because drummers really are certifiably crazy.

2 There's no such thing as a drummer/songwriter.

3 Drummers can be overly sensitive, so treat them with kid drumming gloves.

4 Generally speaking, girls should not play drums.

5 Being a drummer means never having to say you like John Bonham. No kidding. You play the drums, dumbo.

6 Never audition for a band as a drummer and then talk about how well you can sing lead when the band already has a lead singer.

7 If you get a drumstick endorsement, don't take one of those lame promo photos acting like you're biting or breaking the sticks in half.

8 Drummers should never touch the guitars.

The Wisdom of Gear

9 Having band logos on your kick drum only tells the audience that you overestimate your value and underestimate your chances of being replaced.

10 Never put your band's Web site address on the front of the kick drum.

11 Unless you are having an on-tour emergency or just starting out, your drum set must match.

12 If you know how to program a drum machine, you aren't a drummer. You're a computer dweeb.

13 Your drum set should never have a piece of equipment that hasn't been hit in more than a year.

14 Enough with the clear drums already.

15 Never have more toms than hands unless you're insecure about having a tiny penis.

16 Never play a full-sized drum kit while referring to yourself as a "percussionist."

17 No drum stools with chair backs.

18 No plastic or graphite drumsticks.

19 Never have more pieces to your drum kit than you have teeth.

20 No drum key necklaces, especially those shaped like a cross or a Z. If you can't keep up with a drum key, maybe it's time to find a new hobby.

21 Never let your floor tom ride shotgun. That seat is reserved for the kick drum.

22 You can only play a double-bass if you have two kick drums. No cheater pedals on a single drum.

23 Latin percussion should be played only by people fluent in Latin.

Song of the Cymbals

24 Drummers should never have more cymbals than limbs.

25 No cymbals that aren't round. This isn't geometry class.

26 Hardware should be silver or chrome only. Gold or any sort of primary-color hardware is just lame.

27 Wind chimes are never okay unless played on a back porch—and only when it's windy.

28 If you plan to have your hi-hat open and swishing around all the time, then be prepared not to hear any of the actual music and expect to go deaf.

29 Splash cymbals are to be used only as ashtrays.

30 Never use a china crash cymbal, piccolo snare, or vibraslap. A garden-variety cowbell communicates sufficiently to the crowd that you're masking a general inability to play.

31 Never talk about how your cymbals go "pish."

32 You should never "save up" for cymbals. If anything, look for ways to reduce the number you already have.

Song of the Chops

33 A drummer that can play to a click is the drummer to have in the studio.

34 Drummers should learn to play the drums before they learn to twirl the sticks.

35 The grind-core beat is: da-da-da-da-da-da-da-da. The thrash beat is: ta-da-ta-da-ta-da-ta-da. Get it straight.

36 Never use the term "ghost stroking" when referring to your

drum playing. It sounds like you're beating off a ghost.

37 No rolling drumsticks on the floor at a music store to check for their consistency.

The Golden Rules of Attire

38 No drum gloves. If you can't hold on to drumsticks, you may want to rethink the "playing" part of playing drums.

39 All drummers wearing headset microphones should be required to take a food order.

40 The drummer is the only person allowed to wear a bandanna on stage. Especially if he has a full beard and hits his snare like a Hell's Angel hits a hippie with a pool cue.

The Book of Live Performances

41 It is your drum kit. No one must help you carry it unless you pay him/her to do so. However, it is acceptable to befriend at least one unsuspecting sap/fan to carry your hardware bag to the van.

42 No breaking down all the drums on stage and putting them into cases while another band (that people actually paid to see) is waiting to set up.

43 A glossy black kick drum head only means that you're probably gonna be twirling your sticks midsong.

44 Don't polish your cymbals thinking it has anything to do with sound check.

45 Drummers are the only members in the band allowed to bring a rug to play on.

46 This is the drummer's routine during sound check: Play the kick drum now, snare drum now, rack tom now, floor tom now. Good job. You're all done. Now go smoke.

47 No playing drums behind one of those clear fiberglass cages.

48 No cage hardware unless you plan to be locked in said cage.

49 No re-tuning drums during the middle of the performance.

50 No bringing your own Oriental rug on which to play.

51 If you're one of those drummers who set up at the front of the stage, back the hell up. You are the goalies of rock; play your position.

52 In no way, shape, or form will you lead a band from behind your drum set.

53 No drumstick twirling between songs. If you must do that, incorporate it into your playing.

54 No bongo solos unless a bludgeoning of the bongo player immediately follows.

55 Drummers should not pester the sound guy for "more snare out front" during the show. The soundman will more than likely turn the snare mic

off, and he'd be correct to do so.

56 The drummer should never come out from behind the drum set unless it's to leave the stage.

57 No switching drummers during the performance. The crowd doesn't need to see what your band is like with its second-best lineup. Multitasking is for ego-deprived babies.

58 The drummer should always laugh boisterously (while secretly plotting revenge) when the guitarist or singer tells a drummer joke.

59 No making lame "bop-doom-dat-at-at" mouthing while playing.

60 No prearranged smashing of B-grade equipment.

61 If you play with a gong, it should be on fire at all times. Also, you should do everything possible to obtain a flaming mallet with which to strike it. The band is going to kick you out at some point; you might as well go out in style.

62 If you lose "the one," find it before you keep rocking.

63 Two drummers are never better than one.

64 No more showing off blood on the head of your snare that, in reality, came from a tiny cut on your index finger.

65 No complaining the day after a particularly hard show. Shut up and deal with your "bangover."

The Nine Commandments of the Drummer Lifestyle

66 Drummers should never piss off their girlfriends. It's the best way for them to end up homeless.

67 Drummers are the only ones allowed to play wearing shorts (and that's just barely okay).

68 Never purchase a car because you think that the steering wheel makes for a great practice pad.

69 While at your day job, lay off the desktop paradiddles. Your co-workers will thank you. Plus, they really couldn't care less that you're a drummer.

70 While driving, never use cruise control so you can work on your double-kick drum skills.

71 Drummers can be considered gods if they can survive past the age of 35.

72 While you're sleeping with a groupie, remember that when her eyes are closed, she's imagining that she's with another band member.

73 If you decide to keep a drum key on your wallet chain and nobody ever asks to borrow it, start randomly offering it to other drummers.

74 Wash your feet and clip those claws you call toenails before you walk barefoot around the studio floors.

The Complete Resource for

THE GUITAR &
BASS PLAYERS

O N the second day, God said, "Let there be a melody to go between the drums and cymbals to separate drums from the rest of the universe." So God made a six-string instrument and separated the bass sound under the expanse above it by using only four strings. And it was so. God called the expanse "guitar." And there was a power chord, and it should have stayed at that, but God couldn't leave a good thing alone, thus there was a solo, and the solo begat a culture of idiots who were not given enough attention in high school and, as such, loitered all day long in guitar shops testing lots of digital gear that sounded like sandpaper coming out of a dead man's asshole.

The Psalm of the Guitar Player

1 The Fender is rock. The Gibson is slightly louder rock. The Ibanez is ponytail rock.

2 You can never play a Rickenbacker without having your sound described as "jangly."

3 No one cares about the "totally throaty tonality" of one guitar versus "the shimmering high end" of another.

4 Flying V's aren't ironic if you style your hair.

5 Your guitar should not be wood grain.

6 No guitars with strings that aren't in multiples of six.

7 The Gibson SG is the most satanic-looking guitar. It comes with its own set of devil horns.

8 No pointy headstock guitars, unless you plan on stabbing someone in the audience.

9 Never play a double-necked guitar if you're not going to play both necks.

10 The more necks on your guitar, the more likely nobody wants to be in a band with you.

11 Child guitar prodigies have never made good records, no matter what any blues magazine says.

12 Your guitar strap should never be busier than your solos.

13 No one's looking at your guitar strap. Don't ever spend more than the cost of an average meal on something that can be replaced by a particularly hearty piece of string.

14 Boiling your strings may make them sound better, but it also makes you sound cheap.

15 The only people who describe a guitar as an "axe" are dim-witted journalists and over-enthusiastic guitar teachers.

16 The neck of your guitar can't be wider than your upper arm. If it is, you do not play rock music.

17 The more expensive your guitar, the more staggeringly inconsequential your music is destined to be.

18 Play a guitar you're not afraid to drop. No matter how careful you are, it will fall one day. Expensive guitars aren't played by people in real bands; they're played by bank executives at open-mic blues jams.

19 You can't truly rock if your guitar leaves your crotch exposed. Real musicians always hide their junk behind their guitars or basses.

20 Using a bow with a guitar doesn't blow minds.

21 No matter how much you idolize another musician, never put his initials on your guitar.

22 Don't list the make/model/year of your equipment in your record's liner notes. It's a record, not a gear-nerd contest. Save it for when your equipment gets stolen . . . because it will happen.

23 Never use one of those walk-up-and-play-it guitar stands. They make you look like a bigger dope than anyone else playing music, including kids in suburban music shops murdering the classics.

The Wisdom of the Pedal

24 Three words for you new guitarists out there: guitar, cord, amp. Keep it simple, bub.

25 Your guitar should never have more effects pedals than there are band members.

26 If you bring along a light for your pedal board, you might have too many pedals.

27 Volume pedals are for keyboards.

28 Vintage and/or boutique pedals are fine if you want to talk to only dudes after the show. Girls are oblivious to the charms of your pedal board.

The Wisdom of the Amp

29 If you have a wireless system on your guitar, you should test its distance reception by leaving the stage repeatedly during the show.

30 At no time should Peavey amplifiers be used as anything but a place to put drinks or guitar picks.

31 Your amps should never stack up to be taller than anybody in the band. If you can't lift that tube head on your own, you don't deserve it.

32 If your amp has more than six knobs, you are one of them.

The Wisdom of the Pick

33 You should only throw a guitar pick into a crowd if somebody actually wants it. Also, have the courtesy to point to the person once they get it.

34 If you have custom picks with your band name on them, you're most likely in a washed-up band that filled stadiums twenty years ago but is now playing car dealership parking lots and state fairs.

35 Having those plectrum-holding strip things on your microphone stand just tells the world you can't hold a small piece of plastic for 30 minutes.

The Wisdom of Chops

36 Guitar Hero is never a true measure of how "rock" you are.

37 Please understand that every swinging dick that can make a sandwich is a guitar player. You better have the goods.

38 Money spent on guitar lessons is better spent on an in-sink garbage disposal.

39 The guys who win local "guitar god" contests are never in real bands.

40 Dancing or hand gesturing while holding a guitar but not playing it is cause for automatic ejection from the club. Don't get mad at security. You did it to yourself.

41 Don't ever use the term "scales" unless you're referring to (a) a rash, (b) what your dealer uses to measure the 'caine, or (c) a pet snake that should also not be around your neck.

42 Never use the word "chops" unless the word "pork" precedes it.

43 Talking to non-players about playing guitar will solidify you as

someone to avoid at parties.

44 Only "double up" on a tune if there is a riot going on outside and the club is locked from the inside.

The Temple of the Music Store

45 It's best not to try out "classics" while checking out equipment at the music store.

46 Never work at a music store just so you can get "killer deals on gear."

47 Don't ever think that anybody, including the salesperson who sold it to you, cares about your new "rig."

The Book of Live Performances

48 People who wear their guitars too high so they can play faster are always suspect—unless it is a woman who is pregnant.

49 It is never permissible to smash an acoustic instrument unless you've grabbed it from some hippie busker on the street. Smashing an instrument is a reward for rocking out, and acoustic instruments do not rock that hard.

50 Guitar playing requires no special stance.

51 At the end of a show, when you hit the standby switch, that does not mean you do just that as someone

else packs your gear.

52 Hearing your guitar go from E flat to E sharp to E is not a song. Tune your gear at sound check.

53 Either do nothing but jump, or do nothing but play guitar.

54 In the midst of a fast solo, never stare at your fret board, bug your eyes, and mouth the word "Whoa!" The audience does not share your amazement at your mind-bending technique.

55 Rhythm guitar players should always look like they want to be somewhere else.

56 Spraying your fingerboard and hands with WD-40 before the first song will not greatly enhance your playing, but it will greatly impress the crowd.

57 A guitar should never be used as a prop for the lead singer. That's why he has a mic stand.

58 There are only five guitar players in the world who need to change setups more than once per set. You are not one of them.

Golden Rules

59 If you decide to travel to another locale to soak up said locale's historical musical influence, the front door of your new, crappy apartment deserves to be kicked in by that locale's armed drug addicts.

60 Never give lessons as your "main gig" or even as your "side gig."

61 During an audition, never refer to yourself as having "pro gear, pro skills, pro attitude." Musicians who have spouted this motto at auditions have none of the above, especially the skills.

The Psalm of the Bass Player

62 Never, under any circumstances, play a synth bass.

63 Your bass should not, in any way, resemble a bottle of booze or a lightning bolt.

64 A bass should never have more or fewer than four strings. In case you forget, a "six-string bass" is another name for a "guitar." "Someone who plays a six-string bass" may be shortened to "overbearing windbag."

65 Those who figure they will play bass because it has two fewer strings than a guitar and is therefore easier to learn should probably just hold cases that hold guitars and bases.

66 If your bass lacks frets, you lack taste. If your bass lacks a headstock, you're a douchebag.

67 Incorporating an upright bass

into the context of a rock band is just so completely irritating that we can't think of a proper joke for it.

68 If the top of your bass is shaped like the Loch Ness Monster, buy a less stupid-looking bass.

The Wisdom of the Amp

69 The SVT is a completely inarguable piece of equipment.

70 You can have either an active bass or a tube head—never both.

The Wisdom of the Pick

71 Getting plectrums made with your own name on them is a must.

The Wisdom of Chops

72 Aim to be a good bassist and not a talented one.

73 If you play bass in a rock band, you are not a musician. If you want to be a musician and play bass solos, go play jazz.

74 Bass solos have never been a valid form of expression.

75 Never refer to yourself as a "bassist." That implies you are smart enough to handle the two extra strings and have had sex with

people without diseases. Five words: You. Are. The. Bass. Player.

The Book of Live Performances

76 If you're going to play an upright bass during a show, you must play it through the entire show.

77 A bass player can change a string during a show only if a string actually breaks. Even then, it's debatable.

78 No high-slung, goofy bass playing. There is a better way to cover your man boobs. Try a bra. If the body of your bass is rubbing against your collarbone, you accidentally took your little brother's guitar strap.

79 You're probably the most musically educated person in the band. However, unless you're also singing or your bass-playing style has you jumping across the stage, shut up and go stand by the drummer.

80 Never wear a crooked baseball cap unless you're compensating for a crooked head.

The Golden Rules of Stickie Passes

1. AFTERSHOW: Reserved for ladies or acquaintances whom the band doesn't want to see unless there's a million other LIGs (Least Important Guests) around to deflect your inane questions about the recent tour, new album, last time the band played in town, set list, equipment, or online gossip.

2. VIP: The band is obligated to give you a pass but doesn't want to be trapped talking to you before the show.

3. ALL ACCESS: You're more than likely a drug dealer.

4. WORKING PASS: You're either a local slave who's actually working, or your friend in the band forgot about you until the last minute. If you're in Los Angeles or New York, this pass probably means that you're really a band's guest and they actually want to see you.

The Gospel According to

THE SINGER

N the third day, God said, "Let the drums, guitars, and bass guitars be gathered together in meaning, and let words appear." And it was so. The words amalgamated with the melody to produce "vocals." And there were vocals and there was a lead singer. And God saw that it was good, even though his new creation refused to carry any equipment. But vocals allowed bad poets to immortalize their insufferable rantings and gave an outlet to those too untalented to play an instrument. God saw that this was good because the more bad poets who had rock vocalizing as an outlet meant that fewer people would be driven to horrifying mediums like poetry jams and spoken word.

The Wisdom of the Microphone

1 If you sing in a band (even just back-up vocals), bring your own microphone on tour.

2 Few singers are allowed to drape scarves on microphone stands. You are not one of them.

3 No "custom-designed" mic stands made with coyote skulls or lamb femurs.

4 Always use a round base for the mic stand, never a three-legged one. It may be heavier to pick up, but it's much better to roll around with when drunk, and it's a much better weapon for those more unappreciative audience members.

5 Mic stands hold microphones and nothing else. Never bring your own road case. A microphone or harmonica can be carried in your pocket.

6 The only excuse for using a megaphone on stage is if you're a fire marshal.

7 The number of times the mic cable is wrapped around one's fist is directly proportionate to that person's level of meatheadedness.

8 Although your vocal coach showed you how to look cool onstage by grabbing the mic with both hands, reconsider that image.

9 If you break the mic stand, you've bought the mic stand.

Blessed Hymns

10 Vocalists with British accents should be from Britain.

11 Vocalists with southern accents should be from the South.

12 Unless you had hot lava destroy your vocal cords as a child, your affected vocal stylings are completely intolerable.

13 If you rely on a computer to make your vocals sound somewhat tolerable, you should give up singing. Now.

The Good Word

14 Remember that your lyrics might be important to you, but they don't mean anything to anybody else. All that matters is that they sound all right and that you look really good singing them.

15 Unless you've won an actual Pulitzer, you can't write your way out of a dog food commercial.

16 Never have your lyrics ready before you go into the studio. Spend extra money on studio time trying to come up with clever rhymes.

17 If you're the sensitive singer/songwriter type, don't throw in token curse words to prove how edgy you can be. Stick to the things you know, such as how you're the most important person in the coffee shop because you're holding the acoustic guitar.

18 Unless the song ends with "deep in the heart of Texas," don't engage the audience in a clap-along.

19 The word "indigo" has no place in rock lyrics.

20 Any pop song with the word "fuck" in it is a worse song. Any punk song with the same word is a better song.

21 Never rhyme "whiskey" with "miss me."

22 Never rhyme "sorrow" with "tomorrow."

23 Never rhyme "baby" with "maybe."

24 Never rhyme "fire" with "desire."

25 If you mention the specific year/model/make of an automobile in a song, the song must have either three chords or four-part harmonies.

26 Do not refer to "going down," "flying," or "getting farther away" in your lyrics.

27 References to "road," "crossroad," or just traveling in general should also be well reflected on before being committed to paper.

28 A song about being on tour/being on the road/traveling is to a band what a joke about airplanes is to a comedian. It's cheap, it's lazy, and no one cares. If that's the best you can do, maybe you should stay at home more.

29 Writing littered with non-sequitur sentences in parentheses does not make you a literary genius. It just means you got a "B" in creative writing.

30 Nobody is impressed with Charles Bukowski references in your lyrics. You, like every literate person, should have stopped reading Bukowski by age 20 . . . along with Burroughs, Kerouac, and, if you happen to be female, Sylvia Plath.

Preaching on the Mount

31 Whatever your front-man aesthetic, someone did it better already. Probably in the '70s.

32 Remember, you are not these people: Alice Cooper, Iggy Pop, Brian Ferry, or Jim Morrison.

33 Being a great vocalist with loads of stage charisma is incredibly hard to pull off. Chances are, you aren't the person to do it.

34 If you imitate another lead singer, then you're most likely in a cover band.

35 Not even the most outrageous front man should be allowed to play air guitar while the guitar player is playing a solo. Granted, that makes a lot more sense than playing air guitar during a drum solo.

36 Never put anything thrown onstage in your mouth.

37 Your willingness to climb on things does not make you a "good front man." It makes you a "climber."

38 When you feel like stage-diving, first make sure the people in the front like your music enough to catch you.

39 Everybody will know that when you shake up your freebie longneck beer and spray it on the crowd, it is a thinly veiled homosexual act.

40 When you're breaking into a slower song in the middle of your set, always sit on a stool. You'll need something to hold up all that emotion.

41 Don't think about getting naked onstage unless you're either totally in shape or totally obese.

42 Never take off your shirt.

43 You can spit into the crowd if the crowd spits first or if you're feeling particularly misanthropic.

44 If you absolutely want to show how predictable and not "out there" you really are, jump onto a table at your own risk.

45 No fake blood unless you're an old-school glam rocker turned golfer, or if it's Halloween.

46 Only lead singers can handle snakes.

47 Unless you have an above-average stage presence, utilize props, or have a wacky haircut, don't stride onto the stage like you're doing the audience a big favor.

Spreading the Word

48 Witty on-stage banter is intended only for witty people. If you're a boring, unfunny mushmouth in your personal life, you're not suddenly going to become a comedian when you walk on stage. Just shut up and sing.

49 Don't tell the audience how drunk you are. They'll think you're a prick.

50 If you put your finger in your ear when you sing, it makes the audience think that even you don't want to hear your music.

51 Never go out into the audience to sing a song with an audience member unless you're so annoyingly pompous that you feel the need to insincerely "connect."

52 There's no way to overdo pointing. Practice in front of a mirror. Your confidence will skyrocket once you see how cool you look.

53 No written lyrics on stage, by any means, but especially by teleprompter. If you're too old to read or remember your own lyrics, book your next gig at a retirement home.

54 Don't encourage the audience to clap along to your music. Most of the audience members are probably other dudes in lousy bands and keep time like cheap wristwatches. Playing against such retarded, random hand slapping will destroy whatever song you're trying to play. Plus, it just looks plain silly in a 200-capacity club.

55 Don't ever say "Hello, _____" to your hometown in the hopes that it will fool the crowd into thinking that you're some cool band from a cool city. You might fool one person, but your friends know, and they already think you suck and are bitter that they were so bored they had to come pay $5 to watch you play the same stupid songs for the billionth time.

56 Singers who tell the audience to "Give it up for yourselves!" should be attacked by hyenas.

57 Never introduce your slow song as "one for the ladies out there."

58 Never introduce your slow song with "Right now, we're gonna slow it down a little."

59 Using your time on stage to wax philosophical about politics, social justice, and how much better you are than your average audience member makes your live banter little more than a self-absorbed commercial. You should be ignored.

60 Besides singing, saying "thank you," and responding to heckles, you are by no means entitled to explain every forthcoming song to the audience as though they are autistic.

61 There's no need to say "thank you" after each and every song. Buck that trend.

62 There's no need to tell the audience the title of each and every song before you play it. Just hurry up and finish so that people can get back to talking.

63 If you play an instrument and happen to be the lead singer, please, do us all a favor and play your instrument

through the entire show. No song is so important that you need to put down the guitar. Trust me.

64 Don't waste your time during the big closer and introduce individual members of your band.

65 Unless you have a stuttering problem, please refrain from saying your or the band's name between every song.

66 The "front man" of any given band should never complain about the soundman's mix after the halfway-point of said band's live set.

67 Don't ask the crowd if they're "having a good time."

68 No patronizing thank-yous to all the bands on the bill just because they played. Inevitably, you'll mispronounce one of the band's names.

69 No hot, skinny backup singers whose sole purpose is to be on-stage eye candy. Everybody knows it's the fat backup singers whose microphones are actually turned on.

70 No having a two-singer lineup where one sings and the other one either screams or raps.

71 Women should never refer to the rest of their band as "my guys."

72 If you really hate the current political climate as you feel you're supposed to, keep whatever announcements you have to something refreshing and cryptic, or at least self-loathing and ironic.

73 There is nothing more obnoxious than forcing an audience that paid to see you to sing along with your vapid song. Remember, that's your job.

74 Lead singers should pump their fists into the air only during upbeat songs.

The Three Commandments of the Singer Lifestyle

75 You're the one everyone expects will acquire a drug problem. Please make sure that you are actually talented before you do so.

76 Your voice is an instrument. Practice it and take care of it. You don't see drummers pouring beer all over their drum heads or using the kick drum as a bong, so don't do the same thing with your vocal cords.

77 It is artistic felony to have a lead singer who is more than twice the age of anybody else in the band.

78 Your bandmates expect you to live out various sexual escapades so they can experience the rock life vicariously.

Lost Souls

79 "Singers" can sing. "Vocalists" can't.

80 Singers and vocalists are not "writers."

81 No one cares what you have to say.

82 Having a microphone doesn't make you the singer. It makes you the guy who fills in before they find the real singer.

83 When in doubt, it's most likely your fault.

84 Your band (consisting of those people who actually play the instruments) hates you.

85 Remember that you are simply a pale copy of the idea of a street preacher. Act accordingly.

86 Don't show up four hours late to band practice only to storm out because the band started without you.

87 Always have enough peripheral vision so that you don't get in the way of the real musicians.

88 Think long and hard before using the term "front man." Take the word apart and see how that sounds.

The Ten Commandments
of Stage Banter*

1 Shut up and play.

2 Never tell the audience how many songs you have left to play. Although it's considerate of you to give the audience a countdown of how much longer they'll have to endure your horrible music, the fact is that no one really cares. Plus, you always lie. There's always more than one song left.

3 Don't preface a new song by telling the crowd that it's a new song. It's presumptuous to think that everyone is familiar with your material. The chances are pretty good that, for most people in attendance, every song you play is a new song. If you've been around for at least 20 years, your new material sucks anyway.

4 Don't make inside jokes that will be understood only by those on stage at that moment. It's the surest way to make the audience think you are as big a bonehead as you look.

5 Never preach. "Concert" isn't code for "church."

6 Never make more than one reference to the fact that you have records and shirts for sale. More than once makes you look greedy or like you have no short-term memory.

7 Don't try to speak when another member of the band is tuning an instrument or has started a song. If you must say anything at all, wait until it's completely quiet on stage; otherwise, you might as well be speaking Swahili.

---

* Shellac is exempt from these commandments, as they are the only band in the history of rock that's more entertaining on stage when they're not playing music.

8 Thank the opening bands no more than once. Thank the band that's letting you open for them no more than once. Don't thank the nightclub or promoter from the stage at all. Don't thank the audience more than twice. The reason is that, even if you're the sincerest person ever to walk the face of the earth, it will still look like you're sucking up.

9 Never attempt to match wits with hecklers. If someone is heckling you, it's probably because you've broken all these rules and have pissed everyone off. The best way to deal with hecklers is to drown them out with your music. That's what the amps are for, slappy.

10 Shut up and play.

To make things easier for erstwhile activists, clowns, and businesspeople out there, photocopy and tape these commandments to the front of every monitor in the land. The penalty for a first offense will be no sound checks for a week. Second offense: All of your drink tickets will be donated to charity. Third and final offense: Your rock license will be permanently revoked and you will have to busk for change in subway stations for the rest of your days.

The Gospel According to

THE KEYBOARDIST

ON the fourth day, God said, "Let the vocals, drums, and guitars produce a need for more layers of all variety according to various sounds and textures." And it was so. The foundation created keyboards, strings, horns, and a cowbell, bearing even more variations according to their kinds. And God saw that it was good—possibly self-indulgent, but for the most part good. And there was the foundation and there were overdubs and then there was the obvious fact that God had made another mistake, since keyboards, 99 percent of the time, exponentially remove the "rock" aspect of rock and add a level to rock music that can only be described as "gay."

The Wisdom of Gear

1 No keyboards without full-sized keys. Smaller keys are only for Christmas morning, when your parents think a mini keyboard will be your gateway to becoming an accomplished musician.

2 Before you blow next semester's textbook funds on that sweet keyboard you found online, understand the subtle difference between "filling out" and "ruining" a band's sound.

3 No spinning keyboard contraptions.

4 The "keytar" is a waste of plastic utilized by vapid darkwave/'80s rehash bands to assign a nudge-nudge, hardy-har-har sense of irony.

The Book of Live Performances

5 Getting "really into it" on a digital keyboard is akin to breaking a windshield with a wiffle ball bat. All your effort is wasted on a flimsy piece of plastic, and you look like a complete fool to the entire crowd.

6 No playing two keyboards at the same time. Keep your hands on the wheel and shut up.

7 Never play the keyboard intro to any song unless your band really has the guts to play it.

8 No song in the history of rock has ever required a keyboardist to drag their hands back across the keys. Ever.

9 If you're in a fake country band or a paint-by-number garage rock outfit, quit hiding the digital keyboard in the carcass of a broken-down spinet piano. You're not in an off-Broadway musical.

10 There is no upright or grand piano in rock unless it's played while standing up. It is acceptable to play an electric piano while sitting down.

11 Never try to show off your classical training by playing anything by Mozart, Bach, or Beethoven.

Everybody knows you were forced to take piano lessons as a child.

12 Jumping around like an idiot can sometimes make anyone look cool . . . except a keyboard player.

13 There's only one person who will look more ridiculous and offensive in leather pants than the lead singer: the keyboard player.

14 If you play the keyboard with one hand and the tambourine with the other, you are neither a keyboardist nor a tambourine player.

The Golden Rules of the Ineffective Keyboard

15 In the dictionary, next to the word "extraneous" there's a picture of a keyboard.

16 You play a keyboard. "Keys" are the shiny things in your pocket that start the band's van.

17 If you are a keyboard player only, then by no means are you allowed to be in the press photo. You just don't warrant the space.

18 The only reason that we are dealing with keyboards in the context of modern rock is that dilettantes in their early to mid-20s still find mainstream '80s music either amusing or worthy of credible pillage. It is neither.

19 Unless the keyboard player wrote the song, all keyboards are filler.

The Wisdom of the Studio

20 Save the ten-minute, masturbatory synth noodling for your bedroom. Except for you, no one wants to hear it on your album.

21 Any record written by a piano/keyboard player is not nearly as good as the critics say it is.

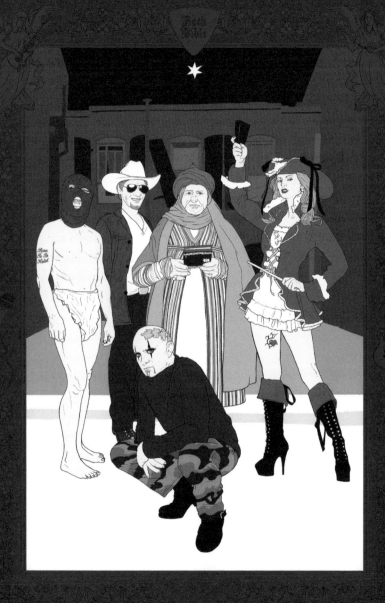

The Gospel According to
THE BAND

O N the fifth day, God said, "Let there be a wholeness in the expanse that was created. Let the drums, guitars, bass guitars, vocals, and sometimes keyboards give sound to the earth." To govern over them, God called the gathering "song." And God saw it was good, even with creative differences. God saw that this was just another version of the dysfunctional family, which God also saw as good because it would give lazy rock journalists something to write about, and there was an album, and then a double gatefold album, and then there was the bargain bin, which served as the final resting place for all albums, and then there was law school, painting houses, graphic design, IT work, bartending, and other service industry work, all rewarding and non-rewarding final resting places for the people who were in bands. And then there was the reunion, and the reunion was to be the most pathetic form of unneeded expression.

The Psalm of the Band

1 Any musician should own and have listened to at least 1,000 records before ever forming a band. Records are cheap. If all you've ever heard is music on the radio or a limited selection of songs from your own generation, you'll never be capable of writing a decent song.

2 You can have a rock alias only if your real name is so truly and irrefutably awful that there is no way you would ever be taken seriously.

3 You can't have a good band without a good drummer, but the drummer always breaks up the band.

4 Unless your last name happens to be Hitler or Daterape, you have no excuse to convert your last name to that of your band's name. Nobody wants to shake hands with Timmy Falsecock.

5 If you ever get annoyed with someone in the band, it's most likely the drummer experiencing what is called a "tempo tantrum."

6 Being a great musician doesn't matter if the music you play is boring.

7 Politics and music don't mix.

8 Be polite to your fans or accept the consequences.

9 No matter how small your band, you will probably have a "super fan" whom you will run into somewhere. Never ever promise to hang out with him or her because he or she will want to pay for everything. More than likely, this small gesture will be something you'll constantly have to repay as time goes on.

10 No band members who play

guitar with their feet or some other freak-show shenanigans like that.

11 Never play your drummer's kit without prior express permission.

12 If you want to be respected as a real musician, no coming within 50 feet of an open-mic night.

13 If a bandmate busts out a click track while practicing in the rehearsal space, leave immediately and never look back.

14 Don't get a homeless person to play in your band. It's hard as hell to find him when you want to practice.

15 Even if you think it will last forever, it won't.

16 There is a fine line between "outsider" music and the exploitation of the mentally handicapped.

17 There is no such thing as too much duct tape.

18 No matter your state or condition, always remember your fellow bandmates' names.

19 Don't hate your younger fans. They continue giving you their parents' money and could manage to destroy your income in a few years.

20 Psychotherapy and rock are mutually exclusive.

21 If you think people are not taking you seriously enough, you're right.

22 If your solo album becomes more successful than your band's last album, just go ahead and quit the band. Save

the lies about "sticking together." Everybody knows you're going to ditch your "friends" very soon.

23 If the only good thing you can come up with to describe a band is that they're nice guys, you'll never

❧ Cardinal Rules ❧

1 No shorts. No baseball hats. No playing the bass with your fingers. And no smiling.

2 Never, under any circumstances, wear your own band's merchandise.

3 You don't get paid to play in front of people. You get paid to sit in a smelly bus or van with your bandmates' collective body funks, listen to your bandmates snore in hotel rooms, eat at Waffle Houses and Mexican joints, load-unload-setup-and-teardown equipment, sit in studios waiting for the guitarists to finally get it right, drink free cheap beer, and drive all night long to get back home to go to work the next day. It's a privilege to play in front of people.

listen to their record in the privacy of your own house.

24 If a member of your band is considering being on a reality television show, offer to drive him to the audition and kick him out of the band along the way.

25 Never get caught reading your own band's press.

26 No one wins a battle of the bands.

27 Nothing will make you less cool than asking your friends/fans to vote for you in a battle of the bands.

28 If you have ever been nominated for an Academy Award, you are not allowed to be in a band.

29 Musicians may not act or model.

30 Models may not sing, play music, or act.

31 Athletic equipment of any kind has no place in rock and roll.

32 If you ever went to Julliard or another world-renowned music school, you must hide this fact from the moment you graduate until the day you die.

33 No matter how bad it gets, just remember that the service industry is always hiring.

34 Never refer to any town's music scene as the next hot spot. Nothing will make it colder quicker.

35 Musicians that move from one musical hotspot to another are as shallow as their own music reflects.

36 No matter how many times you move, your band will always be from the city it started in.

37 The only music style that you can reference the genre in the name is "ska," and everyone knows that all (white) ska bands should be set on fire.

38 If you're considering forming a ska band and you are white, consider forming a polka band instead.

39 If you appear on NPR in any way, you don't rock. Not even a little.

40 If your band has an online-networking page, it's not a band. It's a pedophile.

41 The amount of friends you have on MySpace should be proportionate to the number of records you actually sell.

42 Hair metal clichés stopped being funny in the late '80s.

43 "Conservative punk" is an oxymoron. If you describe yourself as one, you are just a moron.

44 There is not a more pathetic attempt at career invigoration than performing live with an orchestra. Clear them off the stage and save it for the studio.

45 Next time you sing about "being on fire" or "Jesus," bust out the ol' thesaurus.

46 Surf bands should always have a gimmick, even if it's just crazy

outfits. If you are a newer surf band (and not a group of older fat guys who play surf music at parties), your best stage gimmick would be onstage suicide.

47 No matter how much they really like what you do in the band, band members' siblings are not groupies.

48 No bands with siblings, ever. Your family already hates your guts.

49 If you're in a band with your wife/girlfriend, you're not allowed to pretend that she's your sister.

50 You can't hand your band's CD to a successful musician and say, "We're much better than this now."

51 Never hand-deliver your record to the local alt weekly. Doing so merely doubles your chance of not getting it reviewed.

52 Never make an appearance on a local music radio show unless you're absolutely sure it's not the worst program ever.

53 Exceptional players are never born through correspondence courses.

54 Don't ever "know a guy in Nashville," ever.

55 Never be a guy "in Nashville."

56 Never call your band your "music thang."

57 Don't ever use the word "jam" unless referring to backstage rider preservatives.

58 Never have more than one fat member in the band. However, let it be known that one really fat member is a fantastic idea.

59 If your clever band T-shirt concept is to steal the logo of a seminal, underrated/neglected, incredibly hip, long broken-up band, understand that women will not understand it, other guys will ignore it so as not to feed your ego (re: your amazing frame of reference), and general ham 'n' eggers will ask a lot of nagging questions about it.

60 Never describe your new T-shirts as being "pretty cool." They're not.

61 If you're going to be in a death metal band, you must (at the very least) have video footage of your group digging up a coffin. Bonus points are issued if the coffin contains a former member of the band.

62 No practicing at a rent-by-the-hour rehearsal space.

63 Don't ever submit anything to a big music magazine's "Year-End Wrap-Up" because they'll just end up screwing you and then making everyone else laugh at your expense.

64 Parodying *Sgt. Pepper's* has actually been done a couple times already.

65 Remember, the lead singer will eventually become an asshole.

Golden Rules for Naming Your Band

1. Do not name your band after another current band's song or album. Come to think of it, don't name your band after any song or album. Nobody cares about your "good" taste.

2. Never name your band after your personal first and last name and then add an "s" on the end to pretend like you're a group and everyone involved likes the idea.

3. It's always good to name yourself after a large corporate company (preferably an "evil" one) in the hopes that they will sue you later and give you lots of publicity in return.

4. There are no more scary animals, real or fictitious, for bands to name themselves after.

5. Nobody has ever been impressed with really long band names. They're just hard to remember. They assert a quasi-cleverness that will eventually result in most people hating you.

6. When naming your band, think about using adjective-subject, subject, verb, or even adverb-verb. Do not form a complete sentence and do not stick a number in there.

7. Never name your band after a geographical landmark in the city you're from.

8. Don't name a band something you'll get sick of explaining for the rest of the band's existence.

9. Avoid using more than one animal reference in any band name or song title.

10. If you want to name your band something that will be mispronounced by everyone, don't get upset about it when they do. Even your band thinks this is lame.

11 Band or song names should not refer to an instrument in the band. It demystifies the experience, which should be about some zany visual, not a literal, interpretation.

12 There has never been anything "good," "great," "excellent," or "killer" about a band with these words in their name.

13 If you discover that a band in another town also uses your same name, don't hire an attorney. Instead, challenge them to a fight for the name, with a winner-gets-to-rename-the-loser outcome.

14 The only band names worthy of abbreviation are Zeppelin, Sabbath, Halen, Maiden, Priest, and Crüe. Period.

15 Band names taken from children's movies, television shows, or pop culture are forbidden.

16 Never name your band after a food unless you're morbidly obese and it's an integral part of your gimmick.

17 Name your band something so completely preposterous that your music will have to fight an uphill battle against it to convince fans that it's not such a mediocre band name after all. Another plus: It immediately (but temporarily) hides the mediocrity of your music.

18 Adjective–plural noun band names are always most certainly representative of the worst bands. This is compounded if the adjective is followed by a noun that is an animal or a color.

19 All true bluesmen should have "Blind" before their name.

20 No having "youth" in your band name after your 18th birthday.

21 Unless the band is homosexual, the word "fabulous" should not be in a band name.

22 No band names that correspond to weapons from Dungeons & Dragons.

23 Never put punctuation inside a band's name.

24 If you name your band after a person (real or fictional) who is not a member of the band, you are not allowed to complain when people ask which one of you is that person.

25 If your band's name is plucked from some obscure book that only nerdy English majors would know, you have no right to get irritated when asked to explain what it means. Acting uppity because nobody knows the obscure early novels of some French degenerate isn't the correct response.

26 If you name your band after a drug or alcohol, you'd damn well better use that drug or alcohol.

27 Repetitious "word word" or "word word word" combinations are tiresome, and only excessive "word word word word word word word" combinations are acceptable.

28 If you can't fit your band name on a standard-issue nametag, it's too long.

29 You may never name your band after any day of the week, any month or season of the year, any fruit, any adverb, any proper name, numbers that don't signify the number of people in the band, numbers that do signify the number of people in the band, gerunds, any standard color, any plural ending in "z," or any intentional misspelling of a proper word.

66 Unless you're an expert at disguising your voice, never call your radio station's local show to request your own band.

67 Never say, "When I grow up, I want to be in a rock band." Why? Because you can't do both!

68 Stating that you're "big in Europe" means absolutely nothing in the States.

69 Only bands that are not from L.A. say, "We're from L.A.!"

70 No L.A. tour managers who wear their hair in a ponytail, unless you plan on scalping them.

71 Never take anything you do seriously.

72 If you say, "My friend Neil is in that band. I've always wanted to go see them," Neil is not actually your friend.

73 Do not tell people from your day job about your band. They won't like it.

74 "Main" songwriters are the reason everybody else in the band will be working as a dishwasher when the band breaks up. They overvalue themselves and surround themselves with genuinely talented musicians, bring in two chords, and then take all the credit for the entire song.

75 No one cares whom you've opened for, and no one cares whom you've recorded with.

76 Make sure everyone shows up to band practice well fed. Widely ranging blood sugar levels make for the worst possible practice.

77 If you're now in your early twenties and in a band that people seem to care about, consider the complete opposite of that situation and apply it to your late twenties.

78 If what you have to say is currently being said by all the other bands in the press, stop saying it.

79 Find out something that your drummer likes and make sure he gets it regularly. Yes, drummers are poorly evolved creatures, but if you don't have a good drummer who's happy, you're screwed.

80 If you can have a conversation with your fellow band members about something other than your own music, then it's probably worth pursuing.

81 Reclusive artists should always remain that way. Coming out of obscurity ultimately destroys your mystique and shows your few fans that you, indeed, are a horrible performer.

82 Your personal phone can never have a ring tone that is your own band's song. That is identical to going into a restaurant and playing your own song on the jukebox for all to hear.

83 There is no artful way to put skateboarding into a music video.

84 Never have a serious conversation about music unless you are being paid to stand behind the counter at a record store.

85 No eye contact. You're in the rock business. The last thing you need is someone to look you in the eyes and see just exactly how devoid of talent and personality you really are.

Your Band & Their Divine Sound

86 Don't say you're an original band when most of your set consists of unintentional covers.

87 If your band breaks up, stay broken up.

88 Whine, moan, and direct all blame outward when you don't succeed. Even when "they" don't get it, in your own mind you're awesome.

89 Any member of a metal band who states that their music defies category is still in a metal band.

90 Don't confuse the public.

91 It's okay to have a gimmick as long as it's not about how much you love Satan or Jesus.

92 Try to enjoy playing your own original music instead of routinely reacting to trends.

93 The more your band exemplifies contemporary trends, the more likely you'll be forgotten in five years.

94 If your band has a meeting and you all decided whether or not to "get a chick singer," get out now.

95 If your band has regular band meetings, all members should be forced to attend wearing a suit and tie.

96 Use as few words as possible to describe your band.

97 The more hyphens used to describe the genre of music you play, the more schizophrenic and retarded your band is.

98 If you use hyphens to describe the kind of music you play, you are a grammar predicament, not a band.

99 Never be afraid to call it quits. More often than not—the sooner, the better.

100 When asked to cite musical influences, do not cite actual influences; cite your influences' influences.

101 Never get too clever with the influences on "band member wanted" ads. You don't want someone with exactly the same geeky (and untrue) music tastes as you. You hate yourself, that's why you're forming a band, dummy.

102 Never compare your music to classical music. Trained musicians who can actually read music think you're a talentless hack.

103 Never list your influences as other bands you eventually want to tour with.

104 Using the word "jazz" when describing your musical growth is not a sign of maturity.

105 Never play themes from vintage video games. This is not clever.

106 Never describe your music as being "bare bones" or "raw as hell." It translates as either you don't have a bass, you have a girl in the band, or you can't play very well.

107 Never have influences within a decade of the year your band started. If you do, it's to be understood that not enough attention was paid to you when you were a teenager.

108 Never play in a cover band to support your "original" band that sounds like your cover band.

109 Never play in a rock band and tell journalists your main interest is jazz.

110 Cover songs must be at least fifteen years old.

111 Never be white and claim to be playing jazz or blues. You will never do either.

112 If you're going to insist on how much you are influenced by an important record, you must be able to name three songs on that record.

113 Your influences' obscurity is directly proportional to how few people enjoy your band.

114 Never describe your sound as something involving people having nothing to do with music.

115 The awesomeness of a band is inversely proportional to the amount of effects and pedals used to achieve the noises they make.

116 Ironic cover versions are for karaoke singers, and even that's all about ironic hipster smugness.

117 If the bands in your bandmates' record collections are younger than your band, your band is destined to be forgotten sooner than you think.

118 Don't start a new guitar and drum combo unless you're willing to add a bass player.

119 Don't pretend you are better than the Beatles.

120 Don't add something to your band's sound just because everyone else is doing it.

121 Don't let your friends join your band because they think it would be fun if you taught them the guitar.

122 Whatever you call what you're playing, it's neither jazz nor core.

123 Calling a genre anti-something (e.g., anti-folk) really means it is merely a mediocre version of the genre of which it's supposed to be the antithesis.

124 No matter how crazy, wild, or interesting your band is, there is always a band in Japan doing the same thing that makes you guys look like you're standing still.

125 When you do a cover song, don't change it up to show how clever you are.

126 The only place the word "fusion" belongs in music is on that neglected, battery-powered razor in your shaving kit.

127 If your music is ever described as "old school," it is more a reflection of one of your band member's ages than it is a detonation of any true etymology of music.

128 Never claim that you "rock out."

The Wisdom of Gear

129 Playing the spoons as a legitimate instrument in rock is never allowed, especially if the song's lyrics actually mention playing the spoons.

130 You can't play an instrument that is more than ten years older than you.

131 A Macintosh is not a musical instrument. It's a computer or, quite possibly, an apple.

132 Turntables are not, nor have they ever been, a musical instrument.

133 Don't ever touch another man's pedal board.

134 Saxophones and rock never mix well. That's why they call that particular genre "fusion," which is one of the worst permutations of rock ever created.

135 Never be in one of those "collective" bands that have a dedicated xylophone player.

The Golden Rules of Appearance

136 Although a leather jacket might make you look cool, leather pants and a leather vest (not to mention a leather hat) guarantee that you'd look better at a gay bar than a rock club.

137 No snakeskin anything, ever, unless you were once bitten by a rattlesnake.

138 Never spend more time on your hair than you would eating a modest-sized meal.

139 The amount of animal prints worn by a girl in the band is directly proportional to how insane she is.

140 Women should dress like color-blind prostitutes. Men should look like hot women.

141 Don't wear sandals. Look at the floor of an average club to understand why.

142 Unless you're Native American, Mohawks are never a good idea.

143 Never wear matching outfits, unless it's socks worn somewhere besides your feet.

144 If you're a man, wearing make-up increases proportionately to your

inability to play a musical instrument.

145 Unless you're a janitor, no key rings with more than twenty keys.

146 No adult onesies. You should've learned this lesson from high-school wrestling uniforms.

147 Unless you're confused or retarded, you can't wear a scarf or tie with a T-shirt.

148 Never wear makeup and a beard at the same time.

149 The basic T-shirt and jeans look can work for anybody. Venture beyond that at your own risk.

150 If you can afford pants that fit, buy them.

151 Don't be unacceptably indecisive with the issue of going bald. If you have the hairy horseshoe, shave that mess off.

152 Please keep your beards coiffed and trimmed. You are performing for people, and it is important to let them know at least visibly that you care to give them your very best. The first place this thoughtfulness is shown is in your appearance.

153 If your facial hair ends in sculpted points, you most certainly care more about how you look than how you sound. And in case it wasn't apparent, you look like a slack-jawed idiot.

154 If your hair gets more attention than your music, you should wear a hairnet.

155 If you have a tattoo that reads "mayhem," "chaos," etc., across your torso, any girl could kick your skinny ass.

156 A Stax Records T-shirt can be worn only if you can name five artists that didn't have huge hits.

157 No more Revolutionary War stage get-ups unless you plan to reenact a major battle during your set.

158 No calculator watches.

159 No dreadlocks unless you're black.

160 No Beatle boots unless you were actually in the Beatles.

161 If you braid your chin beard, get back to begging for change.

162 Bald heads and makeup don't work well together, but beards and dresses do.

163 No dudes with multiple ear piercings unless you're in a pirate-themed band. However, please, no pirate-themed bands. Pirate culture was never amusing.

164 If there are flames on your jacket, shirt, guitar, drums, amp, or merchandise, you are most certainly in a lousy rockabilly band. However, if the flames are real, and on your head, you must be in a band with a dire need of a gimmick, like claiming to be from outer space.

Visions

165 Don't try to look "tough" in your press photos. If you are tough, you'll look tough anyway, and if you're not, you'll look ridiculous.

166 Never wear a T-shirt of your favorite band to your photo shoot.

167 Never have a band promotional photo taken for which the concept is "urban decay."

168 Never take your publicity shot next to railroad tracks, in an abandoned building, or in a playground. These shots should be taken only in front of burning houses.

169 For promo photos, always look unaffected, staring down and to the right of the camera lens. Crossing arms and leaning against something are also fine, but not at the same time.

The Sixteen Commandments of the Band's Lifestyle

170 If you decide that there's no point in living, don't commit suicide unless you're going to saw your head off with a chainsaw.

171 A "pill habit" is too confusing for most people. Try heroin.

172 Keep smoking. It helps the economy.

173 Recognize the guys who pioneered the music you listen to. Also recognize the drugs they used.

Lastly, recognize the once-important style that you're pilfering.

174 If you write a song about how drugs are bad, you should do more drugs.

175 Only good musicians kill themselves, and if sycophantic rock critics are to be believed, apparently their music gets a lot better after they do.

176 If you want to die while in a famous rock band, there are four options. 1. Suicide. 2. Car or plane crash. 3. Drug overdose. 4. Murdered by a crazy relative. Just pick one and stick with it, and please remember: Deadly diseases are for wimps.

177 Tinnitus is not real. If your ears are ringing, play louder.

178 Dying at twenty-seven is not a rule. It's more like a friendly suggestion.

179 Heroin is acceptable for guitar players and singers, but not for bass players or drummers. They can only be alcoholics or pill-poppers.

180 When you quit drinking and drugs, quit music. It will never be the same.

181 Choose to become drug addicted after you make it big, and not before.

182 Before you speak of "rock" as being an attitude, a lifestyle, a force of nature, or anything other than a type of music, you must have earned a living making rock music for at least ten years.

183 No death by overdose unless you want to be remembered as a pansy.

184 Never pretend you have a chance of making it after having kids if you haven't already made it first. Rocking is one thing that you sacrificed when you decided to have kids. You can't have that life anymore.

185 If you're going to die while choking on vomit, at least make sure it's someone else's.

Temptation

186 Try to avoid inviting ex-girlfriends and potential girlfriends to your shows; you'll inevitably spend more time splitting time than "making up for lost time." By the time your set is done, you'll realize that they are with some other guy.

187 Never date a supermodel/actress with a bigger drug problem than yours. It just takes away from your bad press. Plus, she will steal your stash and eventually end up sleeping with the rest of the band.

188 Your coalescing of porn with your rock band is not edgy, cool, or pushing the envelope. You're simply sullying perfectly good pornography with your lousy music.

189 Unfortunately, most women are fickle enough to fall for any asswipe that picks up a guitar at a party.

190 By the same token, most women also make a romantic career of dating guitar players in active bands. By this, they are displaying their enjoyment in being abused and self-loathed.

191 Everyone knows that women in bands are completely insane, so take it down a notch.

192 Gay or lesbian bands that advertise their sexuality don't rock. Instead, they're a pathetic political movement.

193 Only girls should wear eye makeup.

194 No matter what, every girl you sleep with will have a worse record collection than you.

195 Being in a band won't necessarily get you a date with the female clerk at your local record store.

196 Never sleep with the girl who runs your fan club and can easily destroy your fan-club database.

197 If you form a band with your girlfriend, she'll eventually sleep with everyone in the band except you.

198 The best time to start a band is right after you've been dumped. Creativity and anger often go hand in hand.

199 Don't be a pig and sleep with

your bandmates unless you are in a genuine relationship with one of them. The divide-and-conquer method will only get you fired or break up the band.

200 Limit your vulgar references to genitalia or having sex so that you don't sound like a complete pig. We know you're a pig, but you don't have to make it so obvious.

201 Women in bands will date only guys who are in bands.

The Word of God

202 No Christian bands who use that ambiguous style of backdoor Christianity through vague lyrics and could-be-secular posturing.

203 "Christian punk" is an oxymoron. If you describe you band with this term, you are just a moron.

204 If you are a "Christian" band, you are at least 70–85 percent something other than a "rock" band.

205 If you think God created the world in seven days, you've either spent too much time playing rock music and not enough time in Sunday school, or you've spent too much time in Sunday school and not enough time playing rock music.

206 Save the God nonsense for church. Rock 'n' roll is the Devil's music.

Covenants

207 Never charge people for your band's stickers. If you do, you are also the sort of person who would ask for a quarter when a friend asks for a smoke.

208 "Investing" money is for bankers, not musicians. If you're in need of reminding yourself what rock is all about, knock over a bank, start a chain fight with a teamster, and eat an entire steak soaked in whiskey and cigarette butts. After you've done all that, understand that those acts are a lot cooler than the awful music you make.

209 Your publicist doesn't care about you. The headliner doesn't care about you. The alt-weekly writer doesn't care about you.

210 If you spend more time dealing with record companies than playing in your band, perhaps you should work at a record company instead of playing in a band.

211 If you spend more time manging your band instead of playing in it, perhaps you should be a manager.

212 Never work with an entertainment lawyer who "smoothly" slips you a business card at the same time he is shaking your hand. Actually, never work with lawyers unless it's an absolute must. They are the exact combination of a shark and a turd.

213 If a publicist or record company executive tells you to do something for the exposure, remember that people often die from exposure.

214 Contracts are almost always used against you. Don't sign anything you don't have to.

215 Getting a "buzz" in any city that is not New York or London usually means the end of the band's career is near.

216 No matter how many revolutionary changes are made in the media, the most powerful marketing tool will always be word of mouth.

217 Most labels are looking for originality, marketability, and quality. Not quantity. In other words, they already have that sound. Try again.

218 If you have a famous mother or father and you get a record deal, it's not because you're talented.

219 A famous rock musician who paints or "does art" can only donate his "work" to charity and cannot profit from the sale of his own ego-doodlings.

220 Don't have a "manager" (aka your friend/brother/other relative) before you book your first show. He or she is just there to mooch free drinks.

221 If you frequently mention that your manager has great plans for you, your band will be broken up within three years.

222 Learn the rules about money before you complain about being broke.

223 Don't sign anything you don't understand.

224 Anyone who says he's not in it for the money is in it exclusively for the money.

225 A "sellout" is someone making more money than you.

226 If you are a working musician and not a weekend hobbyist, never complain about how much your monthly take-home paycheck is. No matter how low it is, it's certainly more than you deserve.

227 If someone who doesn't play an instrument is listed as a member of the band (e.g., dancers, stylists, image consultants, and DJs), he/she should be paid as a full member of the band.

228 If you hand out business cards that emphasize your musical ability, you should focus more on the business-card industry than music.

229 If your band puts out press releases, it's not a band. It's a product.

230 Letting your girl/boyfriend be your biggest fan/promoter shows that nobody outside your bed really likes your work.

231 Never write about your own band in any capacity. Just play your

music. Self-manifested publicity is for fools.

232 If your band finds itself recording a jingle for a local television station or business, cancel all your upcoming shows and break up in corporate disgrace.

233 The worst way to reinvent your band is to get the newest, freshest producer on the block to work with you.

234 If you think it would be

Cardinal Rules

1 Never wear your own band's T-shirt. It's never acceptable. Ever. Onstage. Offstage. In your house, smoking grass alone, on laundry day, to the store to buy bread, to the hospital to visit a dying loved one, or even after a tragic fire in which everything was lost except for the band's merchandise in the 4-by-8-foot trailer with barely connected sheet-metal sides. Only heavy metal musicians who released albums between 1975 and 1989 are exempt.

2 Unless you're a drummer, never wear shorts onstage.

---

acceptable to license your music to use in a potato chip commercial but not a car ad, then you're both a moron and a corporate shill.

235 If you really want to make it quick, quit practicing, listening to cool records, and trying to be creative. Put your stock in four cheeseball songs with catchy hooks, get some good-lookin' dudes in your band, and hire some pathetic fan boy to do all the legwork.

236 In casual conversation, mentioning your "latest project" as an "album cycle" reaffirms that you're not in a band, but rather a marketing experiment.

237 No spouses or "significant others" as the band's manager. He or she will inevitably look out for only his/her partner's interests, soon followed by sleeping with another band member.

238 In press releases, avoid describing your band as "[insert seminal act] meets [insert seminal act]."

239 Don't sit around arguing about money, fame, success, and ownership until you can afford an expensive lawyer who will do it for you.

240 Fifty percent of absolutely nothing is absolutely nothing. Percentages, much like promises, mean nothing until you have something worth taking.

241 Jesus may well love you, but get it in writing.

242 Before you sign with a big record label, know that nothing is more embarrassing than a "meet and greet" with local radio-station goobers.

243 Nobody forms a band because they care about music.

244 Never give the drummer any money because he'll just spend it on new cymbals and bad graphic novels.

245 Just because it's done independently doesn't mean you're not being screwed over.

246 Just because one member of the band sets up a few shows doesn't mean that person is the "manager."

The Book of the Live Show

247 Nothing ever starts on time.

The Good Word

248 "Art space" is code for "sounds horrible" and "won't get paid."

249 Calling in sick at your low-paying service job so that your band can play a house party is not "going on the road."

250 "Touring" refers to performing in more than one state

251 Jazz groups and jam bands play "gigs." Punk and indie rock bands play "shows."

252 "Party" is a verb, and if you insist on singing about it onstage, you must demonstrate it after the show, or subsequently participate in a reality show that takes place at an African American girl's college.

253 If your friends are the only people in the audience, it isn't a show. It's show-and-tell.

254 A friend's birthday party is not a show.

255 If it's in a club or bar, it's not a concert. It's a show.

256 If it's at an armory or a community center, it's a show, and you're a hardcore punk band.

257 Actors and dancers "rehearse." Musicians "practice."

The Book of the Tour Bus

258 Never, ever drop a deuce on the bus.

259 On tour, remember that in the van, there's always someone just as hungover as you, so groan a little, drink water, and go to sleep. Telling your band you're hungover is nearly as inexcusable as telling the audience you are drunk.

260 The guy who tracked mud into the practice space will inevitably track mud into the van.

261 While in the van on tour, turn off your cell phone ringer. Nobody wants to hear your ring tone every

Blasphemy: Forbidden Words When Naming Your Band

2	alias	ass	bomb	clown
3	alien	asshole	bone	club
3000	all-stars	Atari	bongo	cold
5	almighty	attack	boogie	collective
'57	alpha	audio	booty	cops
500	altar	auto	box	cowboy
666	altruism	automatic	boy	crank
69	amazing	average	boyfriends	crazy
abstract	American	babies	boys	creeping
aces	amp	baby	brother	crew
acid	anal	bad	buck	crue
acme	analog	band	bucket	crush
acoustic	angel	bastard	burning	cutie
action	angry	beat	butt	cycle
adrenaline	animal	beef	buzz	da
adult	anonymous	bent	cab	daddies
aerial	anti-	big	Cadillac	daddy
aero	apocalypse	bionic	Caesar	dark
African	apollo	birthday	candy	daughter
afro	apple	biscuit	captain	dawg
agenda	aqua	bitch	case	day
agents	arcade	black	cats	dead
air	armored	blind	cave	death
Ajax	army	block	chemical	deer
Alabama	art	blood	children	deluxe
alcohol	ashtray	bloody	circus	demon
alcoholic	asphalt	blues	clean	Detroit

devils	every	funky	head	Johnny
dick	evil	fur	heart	Jones
diesel	ex-	furry	heavy	juice
Dillinger	experience	fuzzy	hedonist	junior
dirt	exploding	galaxy	hell	junkies
dirty	eye	galore	hi-fi	karma
DJ	fabulous	gang	high	kick
doctor	face	garden	hog	kid
dog	factory	gentleman	Hollywood	kids
dolls	faith	Georgia	holocaust	kinda
doom	farm	gerbils	holy	king
dope	fart	ghost	honey	kings
down	fast	girls	horny	kitten
drag	featuring	goat	horses	knife
dream	filth	goblin	hot	knives
drive-by	filthy	god	house	kung fu
drug	five	golden	hungry	large
drum	flaming	grass	hydro	laser
drunk	flash	grave	ice	left
dub	flashback	gravel	imperial	legendary
eagle	flicker	green	incident	lightnin'
east	floating	groove	incredible	lightning
eat	flower	guitar	indigo	li'l
eater	flying	gun	intergalac-	lilac
echo	four	gutter	tic	lizard
elastic	freakin'	gypsy	iron	loco
electra	freaky	habit	jam	loop
electric	free	happy	jazz	lord
electronic	fuck	hard	Jefferson	los
Elvis	fuckin'	hate	Jenny	lounge
engine	funk	hazard	Jesus	love

lust	music	pain	queen	scepter
machine	mutant	panic	radio	scream
mafia	my	parade	rage	screamin'
magic	mystery	part	ragin'	septic
magik	naked	party	raging	sex
magnet	nation	pearl	rain	sexual
man	-nauts	pedophile	raven	sexy
Manson	necro-	penis	rays	shag
master	neon	phat	red	shaved
maximum	new	pigs	retard	she
MC	New York	pimp	revenge	sheep
meat	news	pink	reverend	shot
mega	night	plastic	revival	sick
men	nipple	pop	revue	signal
messiah	Nixon	pork	ring	silver
metal	north	power	ritual	sister
midgets	northern	princess	road	sisters
mob	nuclear	problem	rock	ska
mod	nut	professor	rocket	skank
moist	ocean	project	rockin'	skankin'
monkey	Ohio	psychedelic	rodeo	skid
monster	ol'	psycho	rollin'	sky
moon	old	psychosis	root	slim
morbid	o-matic	pubes	roses	sluts
mother	one	punk	royal	small
motor	orange	puppets	saints	smashing
mountain	orgy	purple	saliva	smegma
mouth	outrageous	pussy	samurai	snakes
mud	overdrive	Q	satan	snatch
muffin	ozark	quartet	satellites	social
murder	pagan	quasi	saw	soft

solid	stiff	tha	trout	wet
son	stone	thang	turbo	whiskey
sonic	strawberry	the	twin	white
soul	sub	thee	twisted	whore
sound	sugar	thrash	two	wild
south	suicide	three	UK	winged
southern	sultan	thunder	ultimate	wolf
Soviet	sun	tiger	ultra	world
space	super	toilet	uncle	worms
special	surf	Tokyo	vampire	X
spirit	swerve	tones	velvet	yankee
sponge	swingers	tongue	volt	yeah
spoon	swinging	tonic	walking	yeast
stand	system	train	warning	young
static	team	trash	wasted	youth
station	teenage	tree	wax	Z
stereo	teeth	tribe	wedding	zen
stick	terror	trio	west	

twenty minutes through five states because your girlfriend at home misses you.

262 The van is not a toy.

263 Don't tour in a bus unless you're sure you can afford it, and don't complain about being broke if you do.

264 Don't paste rock stickers all over your touring vehicle unless you want to give local thieves hints about which car to break into.

265 Always make a schematic of how your equipment best fits in your van or trailer once you figure it out for the first time. This way, even the most meat-headed loaders can help rather than hinder your loading process. It will also help you have the same procedure every night, and it even helps with not forgetting pieces of your gear from town to town.

266 The only food that should be allowed in the band's van is that which can be swallowed. Sunflower seeds are permissible only if you bring a bird on tour.

267 Only closed-type headphones are permitted in the van. No one wants to hear what's bleeding through your headphones over what's playing in the van.

268 If you have a particularly massive gas explosion "on deck," wait until the next stop and do it outside the van. This is called "negating the issue." If it's impossible to wait, roll down the window first, then let it go. This is called "doing the right thing."

269 Keep your eyes open for deer while driving at night. A head-on collision with a deer will ruin a tour.

Sins of the Flesh

270 If you bang a girl in every town you've toured, you're a god. However, a lot of drama can occur if the towns are within 200 miles of each other.

271 When trying to court a female trying to get backstage, offer her a "Tulsa" pass. Tell her that these passes were left over from the Tulsa show but will still work to get her backstage at the show. Please note what "Tulsa" spells backward.

272 If you're married and want to avoid the temptation of sleeping with somebody after the show, simply declare on stage that you want to sleep with everybody in the room. It will guarantee that people will avoid you once you're done playing.

273 If you're on tour and absolutely have to sleep with the first girl you see, tell that unlucky maiden that Jesus sent you.

Cleanliness Is Next to Godliness

274 Wash your clothes on tour, even if you have only one pair of pants.

275 Sexually transmitted diseases don't wash off in the shower.

276 Take showers on tour at least once every three days.

277 Where there are books, there are clean bathrooms. Trying to find a decent place to drop off the kids is tough on tour. Chain bookstores are always a best bet.

278 The worst toilet paper in America is always better than the best toilet paper in Europe. It's best to bring your own, especially to Germany.

279 While driving through particularly hot parts of the country, remember that Menthol powder is your best friend when the van's air conditioning goes out.

280 To save time on tour, open your mind to the concept of the pee bottle. There are just four simple rules. First, this is a good idea only if you have a penis. Second, use wide-mouth bottles (e.g., Snapple), as this prevents unwanted spray. Third, dispose of your bottles at the next stop. Finally, never pee in a bottle that originally held yellow liquid, as the consequences could be less than thirst-quenching.

281 For most backstage toilets, you'll need to travel with your own plunger.

282 Always treat stage injuries immediately after the show. Infection is a greater road foe than diseases or wounds.

Golden Rules for Band Merchandise

283 If you don't sell T-shirts, you don't eat.

284 Unless your touring vehicle has more than six wheels, merchandise shall be limited to T-shirts and records. No hats, pool floaties, or bows and arrows until your driver needs a class B license.

285 Any female that actually buys the thong your band is selling is not someone you want to bring back to the van. And if you're in a band that is selling thongs, go ahead and kill yourself.

286 Stop hawking your merchandise from the stage. If anyone wants to buy a shirt or record, they'll find you when you finally get out of the next band's way.

287 Your merchandise guy is getting action on tour only because he "threw in" a couple of stickers and a T-shirt to the chubby-but-not-too-ugly girl with low self-esteem. It's wise to make him pay you back for the giveaways.

288 Be sure that your merchandise person knows how to make change and can convert currency or barter in a foreign country.

289 If you decide to take elitist scum on the road to sell merchandise for you, you're already cutting your tour proceeds significantly.

290 Personalized license plates of your band's name kill bands.

The Psalm of the Opening Band

291 If you are the opening band, do not play for longer than thirty minutes. Nobody wants to hear that much from you. Plus, if the crowd doesn't get it by then, they never will.

292 Opening bands never get an encore. Play your set and get off the stage quickly.

293 If you are a local band and opening for your favorite artist, do not follow them around all night hounding them to listen to your record. They will hear you soon enough. Try not to suck.

294 An opening band who tells an inattentive crowd to "stick around for the headliner" is being presumptuous but has salvaged a degree of their dignity inversely proportional to the number of audience members who are actually listening to their between-song patter.

295 Unless you're told that the headliner's van has broken down fifty miles outside town, keep your set short. No one takes the freeway just to look at the billboards.

296 Try not to play with bands that sound just like you.

297 Always prank the bands you're on the road with. If you don't have a sense of humor, you'll never survive.

298 If the other band on the bill has brand-new gear, either they live at home with their parents or their parents purchased their equipment.

299 Before you speak ill about another band on the bill, always assume one of their members is in the audience.

300 Don't throw away an opening band's record until you're at the next venue in the next town. There is no telling if they have a friend who works at the club who might see you discard it. It's bad form.

The Wisdom of Gear

301 Never complain about what rental gear you get. No matter what must-haves you listed, you will get what they give you. Every great band that has ever existed has dealt with this problem, so it's not beneath you.

302 Two-guitar change limit during set. Does not include breaking strings.

303 No wireless mics unless you are using them to give play-by-play of your own suicide on stage.

304 Cell phones are never allowed on stage. Not even in your pocket.

305 Old-school microphones onstage are never legit, and mostly sound like crap.

306 When a piece of equipment breaks in the middle of a show, if you look at your road crew/roadie/helper-friend before you look at the piece of equipment, your inability to take care of your own stage mishaps has matched your inability to perform on stage.

307 No candy-apple-red instruments unless you want to look like you're obsessed with candy-apple-coating everything you own.

308 Having two mics taped together is perfectly acceptable. Three mics is even better.

309 You never need more than two guitars on stage per guitarist.

310 No dummy speaker cabinets on stage. All speakers on stage should be wired and have sound coming out of them.

311 Using your computer on stage means you're as likely to be checking your e-mail as you are to be performing music.

312 If there's a Theremin player in the band, they must be dedicated to playing only that instrument during the set.

313 No white blues guys playing a resonator guitar from a rocking chair on stage. On immediate reflection, no white blues guys, period.

Covenants

314 If your band has agreed to do a lengthy tour financed and booked by a corporate sponsor, don't leave home if it starts within the week and they've only booked a handful of dates so far.

315 If you get in a financial pinch while on the road, call your parents.

316 Always wait until after a tour to kick out a struggling or annoying member. Kicking out a member during a tour will only ensure a fight, hard feelings, even more poorly performed shows, and expensive plane tickets home. Be a hero and a diplomat and deal with it for a few more shows.

The Book of Band Popularity

317 If anyone on the tour brings up the bigger show you played the last time you were in town, then they need to shut up and think about that.

318 If your band can't draw five times as many people as are in the band, buy a case of beer and have

The Really Old Testament: Worn-Out Record Review References, Ideas & Phrases

Lo-fi, sonics (as a noun), esoteric, ostensible, sonic (as an adjective), electronica, gangsta, throwback, fuzzy guitars, minimalist, easy listening, prog, distortion soaked, speaker shredding, flotsam and jetsam, ethereal, the next . . . , Sturm und Drang, jazzbo, blistering, magnum opus, genius, old school, patented, ephemeral, pushing the boundaries, reverb, hip (and überhip), sound (as in a band's . . .), resonance, eclectic, -core, multimedia, detritus, bastard child of . . . , spastic, sepulchral, -esque, skronk, ironic, stoner rock, emo, iconic, deliver (bands do not deliver music . . . but they sometimes deliver pizzas), here (a record is not a place), serve up, melds, shards, fretwork, elder statesman, godfather of, gettin' jiggy, phat, cut and paste, click-clack, quirky, quietude, proto-, bid farewell, call it quits, emotional roller coaster, every parent's worst nightmare, firestorm/controversy, hammer out, Herculean effort, haunting, sun drenched, provocative, by the book, punk leanings, rawk, rock, rockin', seminal, incorporate, offer (as a verb for "sell"), toe tapping, shimmer, avant-, guitar lines, brew, elements, group, band, funky, cyber-, effect, affect, beats, eccentric, atmospheric, groove, territory, stylish, 'n', declamatory, lush, aphrodisiac, twisting, tuneful, alterna-, alt-, knack, penchant, prove, melody, new school, psychedelic, abstract, ambient, quality, a sound all their own, impassioned, conjures, reviews that tell you how to play or enjoy the record, myriad, blissful, reviews that guarantee that you'll cry, reviews that guarantee that you will get up and dance, energy, feel, ass, or =, kicking it, recall, anything with "ear," aural, unabashed, evocative, allusions to musician's criminal record, collections, decidedly, drop (as an adjective or verb), moody, plaintive, heartbreak, reminiscent, in a big way, tweak, croon, coo, pop sensibilities, vibe, junkie blues, references to enjoyment of beverage or narcotic while listening to, album, vinyl, turntable, smooth jams or grooves, keeping it real, blunts, full-throttle, 1977, voice of a generation, finger on the pulse, punchy, bling bling, shoe gaze, up-tempo rocker, well-crafted pop, bombastic, dissonant, icy grill, edgy, architecture, pop duo, poet, wordsmith, diva, smokin', hard rock, chops, licks, reviews stating how the album is great for listening to in the car in summer with the top down, kids, stew, musings, inventive, shambling, sexy, kittenish, uninspired noodling, jagged guitar, buzz-saw guitars, flux, high concept, classically trained, aptly titled, infrequent bedfellows, ravishing, veteran, flounders, thirty-something, soundtrack for . . . , iconoclastic, hummable, hippified, foot-stompin', ex-, legend, on target, showdown, split personality, solid, betrayal, tasteful, crossover, burbling, feverish, alumni, culls, proper, until now, wunderkind, operatic, loneliness, loose, angular, diverting attention, grandstand, ingénue, electronic, disenchanted, scruffy, experimental, spaghetti western, drunken, ultra-, bleak, craft, recycling, wonderfully bizarre, willful, clichéd, floating, stint, futuristic, dope, dreamy, acid folk, organic, collision of, nostalgia, montage, remorse, nasally, wash, cut up, new wave, nightmare, solo, screwed up, eponymous, soundscape, any

throw-away journalistic adjective used by any on-line critic, underground, indie, odds 'n', sods, under the radar, off
the map, stylings, force, touching, unsentimental, tinker,
harmony, full length, crashing drums, . . . and crew, over-
compensate, fuzz, distant, ebbk, squashing, mayhem,
swooning, agonizingly, sophomoric, braggadocio, svengali,
sophomore effort, sophomore slump, whiskey-soaked, roots
rock, post-, conquer, era, return to form, atmosphere, -y,
acid-soaked, making everyone their bitch, neo-, somnolent,
derivative, lysergic, drenched, steeped, Southern-fried
(referring to music), from Louisiana as food from the
region, love-child, drops, will drop, tasty licks, searing,
licks, good music to (insert verb) to, my advance copy . . . ,
sure to be a hit on the dance floor, really jams, departure,
insightful lyrics, impressive debut, better than . . .

whatever audience you can get come watch you play at your rehearsal space.

319 Packing out your show by inviting your entire extended family does not mean your band is massive, nor does it give you license to argue for free entry at the local nightclub.

320 If your band is drawing more than 80 percent dudes, you should break up and go into weightlifting.

321 Stop blaming the promoter, the booking agent, the club, and the label. Instead, start blaming yourself.

322 If you're playing small venues after headlining arenas, save your fans the "we wanted to get back in touch with our fans, smell the sweat, see the faces" stuff. Just admit that you're not as popular as you used to be and then move on. And in this case, "move on" means break up.

323 If you're unsigned and without a booking agent, free music festivals hate you and your struggling band. Nonetheless, they will still gladly take your entrance-fee money as a sort of "idiot tax."

324 If your band has hired a film crew to document your perform-ance and you draw fewer people than are in said crew, pack up your van and go home.

The Golden Rules of Promoting Shows

325 Never ask a venue about booking another show while a mem-ber of your band is being escorted out by security.

326 If your band just formed a month ago, don't ask that guy who books shows at the local club to "book a tour" for you because he might "know people."

327 If you require a booking agent, hire only those who have actually been on tour. They will know the merits of good routing and the perils of bad.

328 You cannot include a reprint of a record review in a show poster.

329 Unless you're just starting out, playing your hometown more than three times a year is best left to cover bands.

The Word of the Prophets

330 If promoters ever double-book a show on your band, you're allowed to club them with this book until they can no longer move.

331 When the promoter tells you the van will be fine in that No Parking zone, it will get a ticket.

332 If the promoter starts off a con-versation with something along the lines of, "So, about this guarantee,"

you're completely justified in stealing any equipment from the club. Consider stealing the 8-balls in the club's pool tables first.

333 Never accept beer as payment from the club or promoter unless the entire band is filled with raging alcoholics.

334 The worst club in Europe is always better than the nicest club in America.

Disciples

335 If you can stretch your limits far enough to say "hello," "please," "thank you," and "goodbye" to the sound man and the other bands on your bill, such niceties will make your life a lot more interesting (and maybe even a little longer) than anything produced as a function of your well-worked "attitude."

336 If your tour manager dresses like the band or has an identical haircut to a band member's, then said manager must be kept in the production office as much as possible.

337 Anyone riding with the band is required to load and unload equipment.

338 Ensure that your tour-bus driver is everything you're not: sober, muscular, nice smelling, law abiding, and uninterested in prostitutes.

339 If you decide to hire someone to do sound or lights for you, let him

do it. You can not tell how it sounds or looks to the audience from where you're standing, so don't pretend like you can. If the sound or lights aren't good, then it's your fault for hiring someone who can't do the job.

340 Never let your "buddy" tour-manage unless he knows what the back end is.

341 Don't yell at your stage crew; they have the power to pull the plug on any one of you at any moment.

342 Do not take to constantly criticizing your sound man's ability during a tour. No matter how funny you think it is, at some point during the tour, he will begin to consciously cripple your future.

343 If you're in a band with more than one useless member, always head-count members at every stop. That will save you from getting a call shortly after you start driving and having to turn around to pick up whoever Joe-drag-their-ass is in your band.

Spreading the Word

344 Be sure to have one of those enormous Rand McNally maps and at least one person in the band who knows his elbow from the interstate. Online map programs will only keep your van driving in circles.

345 If you want to get out of driving a night shift, wait until everyone

is asleep, slam on the brakes, and then announce to everyone you're dozing off and are afraid you'll kill everyone. Their hearts will be racing and someone will be wide-awake enough to drive. Then, you can crawl in a comfortable spot in the van and get some good, sound sleep.

346 As soon as you go on your first tour, put a piece of duct tape above the driver's side visor that is marked with everyone's initials. It will serve as your permanent driver rotation. Anyone who misses one of his shifts will have to endure a double shift. This is one of the simplest and most time-tested rules of the road.

347 Seriously reconsider bringing your dog (or any pet, for that matter) on the road. It is rather cruel to the dog, your van will smell like dog food, and one of your dumb-ass bandmates will inevitably lose the dog somewhere along the way.

348 As tempting as it is, don't speak in "in-joke-ese" around everyone you meet while on tour. They'll quickly realize that you're a self-absorbed boob.

349 Always "idiot check" after the show, no matter how drunk you might be. There's no telling what you left in the dressing room, on stage, or somewhere in the club. Sometimes you're lucky just to get all the humans in the van.

The Wisdom of Load In

350 When asked what band you are upon arriving at the club, respond with "the one that rocks."

351 Load in is hard to time just right unless you have a hard-ass tour manager. Usually, you're really late or waiting outside the club for some goofball promoter to show up and let you in. Always be stocked on books, magazines, movies, and general downtime diverters, or you'll lose your sanity after about a week on the road.

352 Bands that can't set up quickly cannot possibly be good.

The Wisdom of the Sound Check

353 Sound check isn't a goodness check. If it were, you would probably have flunked it.

354 A sound check is the bit where you check to make sure the sound is going to be okay. It's not your next rehearsal.

355 Never expect to get a sound check when you are the middle of three bands.

356 Sound checks should never last more than one hour.

357 No man-bags sitting on top of amps during sound check.

358 Learn the sound guy's name before sound check.

Behind the Altar

359 Never plaster the toilets with your band's stickers unless you want the public to equate your band name with going to the bathroom in a really disgusting place.

360 When you see a band's sticker on the sweet spot of a urinal, don't put your band's sticker over it. It's not the kind of promotion you want.

361 The worst bands always write their own names on the wall backstage.

362 When you write your band's name on the wall of a dressing room, the next band in there will write "sucks" next to it. Spare yourself.

363 Never make a mother and daughter both show you their breasts to get backstage. It's tacky.

364 From the second they were delivered, backstage couches at rock clubs are never cleaned. Think of the crazy things that have been done on or near these couches and then proceed at great personal risk.

365 There can be no backstage dressing room without a crudely drawn penis on the wall. If you don't see one, immediately draw one on said wall.

366 No one is allowed backstage without a pass unless they're hot or have drugs for the band.

367 All-access passes look idiotic in small clubs. If there's no backstage, you don't need a backstage pass.

368 Memorize this phrase, it will serve you well: "No, I will not get you backstage."

The Wisdom of the Rider

369 Never put condoms on your rider.

370 Don't try to write the "funniest" rider ever. They're never as good as you think and typically lead to band humiliation.

371 It's always best to request more booze on your rider than you'll actually need. Plan on having an extensive liquor cabinet once you are dropped from your label.

372 Asking for ointments on your rider is a good way to both creep out the promoter and quickly reach legendary status.

373 If you're a vegetarian, don't trust the promoter to feed you. You'll be lucky enough to trust them to give you your guarantee, let alone food without meat in it. Better yet, if you're a vegetarian, don't go on tour.

374 Drink tickets may be made of paper, but divide them up like they're gold. They might be the most you'll ever get out of a club.

375 If you're playing at a venue that agreed to feed you, tell them to

The Golden Rules of Laminates

Laminates are a very popular form of ID. Here's how to tell who's who.

1. HUNG AROUND THE NECK: This person does not belong anywhere near the stage or dressing rooms. Identify him as a poseur and don't even offer him water.

2. HUNG FROM THE BELT: This person may work for the band or it may be a laminate from a completely different show. There's still the possibility that he is a poseur. Offer him the deli tray only.

3. IF A LAMINATE FROM ANOTHER SHOW IS VISIBLE: This is otherwise known as "resume on a rope." This person is immediately classified as a poseur. Do not pass dressing room; do not collect hummus.

4. IF A LAMINATE FROM A PREVIOUS TOUR IS VISIBLE: This person blew it at the after-show the last time and the band still doesn't want to see his or her face this time around.

5. IF A LAMINATE IS CONCEALED OR STILL ON THE HOTEL BED: This person probably actually needs one but is still probably a poseur. The only difference is that he's getting paid tonight.

order something other than pizza, because you'll be eating a lot of pizza on tour.

376 Keep dietary choices out of music. You're not special.

377 It's a great feeling to have a rider, but be careful how many joke items are on it. A baggie full of cinnamon is one thing, but a bathtub full of mulled cider comes out of your guarantee.

378 Strip those crummy riders out of your contracts and pack your own white towels and energy drinks.

379 Asking for socks on your rider is a good idea, but you'll rarely get them. Purchase a cheap package of socks that you can throw away after each performance. The overall effect is better-smelling feet, which equals a much better smelling van.

Through Heaven's Gates

380 No guest list for journalists, ever. If they don't want to pay to get in, they don't like your band enough to write something good about it.

381 If you can be courageous enough to go with a no-guest-list-for-anyone-ever rule, you will be making sure that only people who truly want to see your band will be the ones who show up to see you play. In the long run, this strategy will prove to be a very good thing.

382 No guest lists at benefit shows.

The Wisdom of Pre-Show

383 Before hitting the stage, do not have a group huddle/prayer session with your bandmates, especially when the other bands on the bill are in the dressing room. They will correctly assume that your band should be ignored.

384 No pre-show warm-ups or athletic-style stretches.

385 When arriving at a club, avoid any manual labor by urgently leaping out of the van screaming that you have diarrhea, running to the bathroom (spending a few minutes there), saying hello to everyone in the club, getting a drink at the bar, and starting a conversation with the barman. Then, return to begin sound check and divert attention with: "Hey, I got us our drink tickets!"

386 Don't get caught pumping iron in the "green room" right before going on stage.

387 Doing stretches or jumping jacks on stage before you play tells the audience that something bad-ass isn't about to happen.

388 Don't wait until the last minute before you go on to burn one from the band's communal pipe. Then, don't make the crowd sit

through your residual coughing and wheezing. Plus, pot is a bush-league drug designed for suckers.

389 You can never come on stage like a rock god if, moments before, you were setting up your own equipment.

390 Never try to play along with the house music while you're setting up or waiting to start your set.

391 Having someone come out to "pump up the audience" and introduce your band for anything less than a stadium of people is a juvenile attempt at "playing" arena rock.

The Wisdom of Onstage Appearance

392 For their pretentiousness alone, anyone in a fur coat onstage should be set on fire.

393 Any member of a band wearing a heavy coat onstage at an indoor gig, unless he's in an igloo, is more likely to be a fashion model than a musician.

394 Bands that wear suits should never do summer tours.

395 You cannot rock while wearing a rubber bracelet.

396 You should never have a music stand on stage.

397 Headbands can never be worn on stage. If you do, you're either a bloated has-been or a trendy action figure. Wristbands, however, are completely acceptable.

398 Unless you're sitting on a horse, lose the cowboy hat.

399 Don't smoke when you're actively playing your instrument during a performance. Many have tried before you and failed to make this look natural.

400 Never be the guy in a band who wears a ski cap on stage. As you'll undoubtedly find out, house-lights do not have a cooling effect.

401 Middle-aged men in bunny suits on stage are not entertainers, they're borderline pedophiles.

402 Always wear shoes on stage. Sandals don't count as shoes. Nobody wants to see your feet.

403 Always keep your shirt on.

404 Don't wear black. Even if you're fat. It makes you look like you have a disembodied head. People only want to see disembodied heads if there is blood dripping from them.

405 Unless you actually beat your wife, wearing wife-beaters on stage is strictly forbidden.

406 If you need to wear glasses on stage, they should stay on without the help of a sports strap.

407 Wearing earplugs anytime, anywhere is an admission that you are too old for rock and roll.

408 Unless your ringing ears hinder performances, decibel-reducing headphones are not allowed on stage.

409 Men can't wear women's clothing on stage if they, indeed, look like women.

410 Unless you're performing directly facing the sun, hats, sunglasses, or bandanas are never allowed.

411 No white belts unless you had a karate match immediately preceding the show.

412 Your tour should never require as much hairspray and/or makeup (in total weight) as musical instruments.

413 You're not allowed to have stage-only clothes.

414 Bands that dress up onstage in pop-culture-friendly costumes should be required to run children's daycare centers.

The Golden Rules of Onstage Antics

415 If you can't make the ground you land on after your well-practiced precision jump splatter water in slow motion, then please do not include this effect in your band's video.

416 The space between songs is intended for grabbing a quick drink, talking to the crowd, or silently tuning up. It's not intended for you to sit there and practice that great lick you just thought of or to "telegraph" the sweet lead part of the next song you are about to play. All that does is tell the crowd what song is coming up next, and that's entirely unprofessional.

417 Air keyboard is never acceptable on stage, even as a joke. In fact, no "air" anything. Ever.

418 Dramatically drinking a beer from the stage is neither witty nor intense. Keep in mind that every audience member also has a beer that they're most likely drinking.

419 Never be known as a band that has band drama unfold on stage.

420 Hand signs are only for the mute.

421 A band should never smash its equipment at the closing of every show on any given tour, regardless of attendance.

422 Unless you're in a band with all girls, you should never average more than one piece of clothing to be taken off per song.

423 No electric fans on stage. They may cool you off, but they make you look like a fruitcake.

424 Head-banging is for metal bands and no one else.

425 Don't throw feces at your fans. They'll love it, but you'll go to jail.

426 Only the truly gullible are fooled when you smash your instruments at the end of your set after you've stood on stage staring at the floor the entire time.

427 Being wasted onstage works for only about 5 percent of bands, and yours isn't one of them.

428 You are never allowed to eat solid foods onstage unless you're morbidly obese.

429 Never count off songs doing "one-two-three-four" in other languages, other number orders, or other witty substitutions.

430 Bringing crowd members on stage should be followed only with you leaving the stage for the night.

431 Pointing at other band members while they solo or posture is strictly forbidden.

432 Never tune audibly onstage. If you don't have the common courtesy to buy a tuning pedal, then we would just as soon not pay five bucks to hear you noodle on the pentatonic scale.

433 It is permissible for someone in the audience to shoot guitarists onstage asking one another things like "Lemme hear your A string, man."

434 All authentic stage props must be inflatable.

435 No taking photos of the crowd from on stage. It's cheesy and is a cheap excuse to remember your post-show conquests from stage perspective.

436 No switching instruments just to show you can. One lineup will always be stronger.

437 No doubling up on a mic. It looks like you're sharing an ice cream cone and is completely amateurish and unflattering. Spring for the extra microphone, you cheap so-and-so.

438 Don't throw hissy fits on stage. Nothing is ever as important as you think it is.

The Wisdom of Your Set

439 If you actually have some hit songs, never open your concert drunk off your ass doing covers of Elvis and Lynyrd Skynyrd and not doing the songs people know.

440 If you don't want to play any songs from your first three records, then start a new band and call it something else. You don't get to sell tickets on the old hits and not play them.

441 Never make a set list that has an "encore" written on it.

442 Never begin an encore with a new song. It's like punting on third down.

Your Sins

443 If you make a little mistake, never stop and restart your song. Keep going. The crowd doesn't care.

444 Never make excuses for screwing up onstage.

445 Never apologize for a poor performance during your set unless you're willing to refund people's money from the stage.

Talking Onstage

446 During a set, you can't say "We got one more for ya," because everyone knows that means "We got four more for ya."

447 Never converse with fellow band members on the microphones between songs.

448 Never ironically tip your hat to hip-hop on stage because it will show that you are doing one of three things: apologizing for being white, secretly wanting to be black, or feeling that you need to divert your complete lack of soul. People always see through this ruse.

449 Rock 'n' roll and dedicating a song to any friend or family member are mutually exclusive.

450 Don't mention more than once that you have "merch" for sale. Better still, don't mention it at all.

451 All of Cincinnati isn't here, so please don't say hello to them. Also, this is one of the worst jokes ever.

452 Saying "Don't forget to tip the bartenders" always gets you more free beer than was originally agreed upon.

453 It's never appropriate to say "This is a little song we call tuning."

454 If you spend significant time onstage having a Q&A session, you're not a band; you're a comedy act.

455 Asking the audience to partic-ipate in your song will show that the majority of them have no musical ability whatsoever.

456 Don't beg for audience members to buy you drinks while you're on stage unless it's your birthday.

457 Scolding your audience for talking during your performance will only help alienate your fans and encourage fewer people to come to your next show.

458 Never ridicule the staff of any performance venue unless said staff has threatened intentional spreading of herpes.

459 Don't lip-sync along with your own samples between songs. We all know that you're just a robot incapable of original thought.

460 Never do anything to encourage the crowd to pull out lighters unless you're playing a ballad for more than six thousand people, or you just instructed the audience to set a heckler on fire.

461 Remember that whenever you name-check a band, there are dozens of people in the room who think that band isn't that great.

462 Never ask for drugs between songs unless you plan on doing them while everybody watches.

463 If the crowd looks bored, then they probably are. Change up your pitch.

464 Never attempt to retell jokes from the movie *This Is Spinal Tap* while on stage.

465 Refrain from asking the audience how everything sounds after the first song.

466 If you are a band full of guys and your singer introduces a song as being about rape, it better be about someone in your band and his experience in a maximum-security prison.

467 The less popular your band is, the number of times you are allowed to say a city's name drops exponentially.

468 If you ever ask the crowd what song they want to hear next, be fully prepared to hear "Your last!" shouted back at you.

469 Never invite people in the crowd onstage to dance while your band plays.

470 A band should never reference its various members' nonmusical credentials while onstage.

The Sound on Stage

471 If your live show sounds just like the record, then you have just wasted the audience's money and time. You're not that good-looking.

472 Never ask somebody standing on the side of the stage who's been drinking your rider for the entire show how you looked or sounded. If you do, you'd probably have as much

common sense to call your therapist when your kitchen sink is clogged.

473 Before asking the sound man for more of something in your monitor, take the time to check whether there are actually any monitors present.

474 Nine out of ten clubs have horrible sound systems, so it's more than likely nobody is making heads or tails of your lyrics anyway. Just make sure you're in rhythm and the guitarist's monitor is turned down so your screams don't pierce his already shredded eardrums.

475 If you have to ask the sound man for more vocals in the monitors more than once, accept that you're not going to get it. Stop asking. Stop making the "turn it up" gesture. Just suck it up and play.

476 After the first song, always ask for more of something in the monitors. Doing so ensures that the sound man is actually working and not drinking at the bar.

477 When you're in the midst of a bad show, don't start complaining about the monitor mix. An eight-year-old can see through that trick.

478 If the sound guy is being assertive about having you play only one more song, proceed to play an improvised opus that lasts an hour. If the power is cut off, it's time for a drum solo.

479 Never allow the sound guy to control samples or any sounds from the booth.

480 During the set, make yourself appear to be an expert by pointing at the monitor, then at the bass player, then point up. Girls find that both hot and also somewhat perplexing.

481 If you can't hear yourself in the monitor, that should be a big hint.

482 Never let a house sound guy "dial" something in.

483 Be nice to house sound engineers. They will still be working in the music industry when you have to go back to waiting tables.

The Golden Rules of Show Production

484 If your live show is so weak that you need to show low-rent arthouse videos projected behind you, do not perform live.

485 It doesn't bode well when a band allows the lead singer to control the rest of the band's lighting via footswitch.

486 If you have to be loud to sound good, you're grossly overcompensating for your lack of talent.

487 If your band doesn't like performing live, reconsider doing it. If you enjoy taking people's money and just going through the motions, you're not a musician. You're a prostitute.

488 The bigger the light show, the worse the band.

489 Always ask the crowd if they can handle more explosions. In the event that they are unable to, you'll probably want to scale back on the flare cannons.

490 If your live show requires a set change, you're not a musician. You're doing musical theater.

491 If your live show requires a costume change and your act isn't low-budget theater, you're not a musician. You're a fashion model.

Water & Wine

492 Drink iced tea from whiskey bottles. It allows the crowd to think that you can play flawlessly while drunk.

493 No sports drinks or soda on stage, ever. Beer. Water. Whiskey. Only.

494 No wine can ever be drunk from wineglasses.

495 Getting really drunk and adding what you consider "great ideas" during your live performance is the pinnacle of self-indulgence and will alienate your fans.

496 If you're in a band that's known for drinking excessively during your performances, your audience is doing you a disservice by not administering an intervention.

497 For every bottle of water the audience sees you drink onstage, they must also witness you drinking three bottles of beer or they will think you are either in Alcoholics Anonymous, pussies, or Christian rockers in disguise.

False Hymns

498 Never open with a cover.

499 If your band covers a song that no one in the audience recognizes, it does not mean you are cool, it means you covered a bad song. Obscure never equals good.

500 Performing a non-reggae version of a reggae song just reaffirms that you're a white kid who grew up in the suburbs. Additionally, you should never do a reggae version of anything.

501 When playing a cover, please refrain from spouting off about how much the covered band means to you. No one needs to know to what extent you are a hapless little fanboy.

The Wisdom of Post-Show

502 If, after getting off stage, you ask a friend what they thought of your show and they say, "You guys were loud!" or "You guys were tight!" they are politely trying to say that you stink.

503 Loading off is not a performance. Get off stage like there's another band waiting to go on, because there is.

504 If you get back to the hotel or place you're crashing after the show and find you still have unused drink tickets in your pocket, you have failed.

The Day of Rest

505 If you're crashing on some kind soul's floor, make sure their male cat is kind as well. That is, unless you don't mind your sleeping bag smelling like cat urine for the rest of the tour.

506 If you can, always splurge for a slightly better motel. The beds are more comfortable, the staff will allow you to sleep in, there are more channels on the television, and the water pressure is always stronger.

507 When staying at someone's house, be courteous in the shower line. Hot water goes quickly, especially if it's some kid's rental dump.

508 When staying at squats in Europe, keep your hooded sweatshirt cinched up tight, try to sleep with your hands in your pockets, and, whatever you do, hide your wallet.

509 Get the hotel room right by the elevator so you just have to remember a floor, not a number. It's also acceptable to take a red marker and copy your room number onto the side of the ice machine.

Underused Words for Critics

Splayed, niggardly, funkateer, bukkake, MILF-damaged, engorged, dilated, spiffy, hole-filling, basic needs bass knees, barnacled, aggregate aggression, tandem drumsticks, mic milking, misunderestimated, doobied, fiddle faddle (as a verb), douchebaggery, flappy, toodly, twinkish, crotchety, pissy, farty, snippy, snooty, root-too-tooty-fied, Chester-fried, scum-bummed, glorping, mung, re-virginized, sloppy scarf rawk, Haskell-esque, Snatch-22, mock-rock, dubious, Richard Dreyfus (as either a verb or an adjective), full-on rock-and-roll facial, flaccid, balls-out, goose-pimpled, beige, brownness, barfy, diarrhea, tripe, crap, shit, awful, fucking awful, really fucking awful, rip off, ripping off, stolen, blatantly ripped off, low-ball, low-balled, diar-rhetoric, stupid, pointless, jugular, fisted, payola, lawsuit, gamey, goy band, rapey, pube ring, galoot, filched, chinwag, squishy, nut-punchingly good, nut-punchingly bad, hits like a battering ram (but only when applied to acoustic and/or folk music), ridonkulous, cat-box fodder, a, musical donkey-punch, painful rectal itch, ironical, causes temporary gayness, bris-tastic, scab-rock, grudgefuck, urine-tasting, meat-beatingly good, balls-in DVDA, back-end (instead of low-end or bottom-end), poop decks, sebaceous, tittyish, leg warmer, aphasia-inducing, fucktarded, Albini-less, bandtastic, balls-in, dirked, eastern block, faminesque, flugelhorn, gaussian, hussified, linebacker, out-hustled, salty, seltzers, smurfy, slamma jamma, that "Scranton Sound," troop supporting, zoomy, golly wolly doodle (as a verb or an adjective), undergood, fissured, unlegendary, earth-wiggling, mind-fumbling, dick-quaking, mouth-hosing, cock-tapping, pussy-juggling, ass-taunting, snot-guzzling, hippie-awakening, goodly, penurious, sparky, li'l squeaky, Turing-tested, Hawking-approved, gumption, nut out the window, dunder-headed lummox, trailer-park troglodyte, dog feeders, pencil titties, words that rhyme with Funyuns, Heitkotter, worse than Hitler, Owings-approved, ramen, bell-end, Post-Pre-Prototype Christian IKEA Rap, hailing From Utah, . . . whose members all share convictions stemming from the *Dateline NBC* "To Catch A Predator" TV series, fagmo, gelatinous, carpetbagging, Nipsey, jizzed, re-jizzed, re-smegmanated, simonized, reverse engineered, remotely viewed, transmo-grified, Dimebaggedly, Kevorkianated, turdly, twinked, gayed-up, crotch-splitting, premature birth-inducing, grandmotherly, sheetrock, Iowa, punctual, prosthetic, phlegmatic, hirsute, dandy, secretarial, incestify, boob-worthy, amp sandwich, sucka' bassoonist, post-good, punk-jock, coistered, cold-filtered, feltch-worthy, penis-gouging, -esque-er-ing-ly-able, coco, honkey-enabling, white bread Fred, sperm-burping, Whisker Biscuit-like, "that's very white of them," faggotry, faggot-like, smokes pole, bedrag-gled, post-wallet chain rock, post-flame detail rock, bassoon-fueled, masturbation-defying, free polka, Eastery, tumoriffic, way spanky, Eugenetic!, Tiny Tim Hum Drum, ginormous, Convertible, results-oriented, Volvo-esque, kinky, formally rational, well-insured, moisturized, fruit-filled, lightly scented, all trippy'n'shit, alabaster, quaintly hetero, patient as a stalker, jock jamz, razzle-dazzle, toothy, well-tanned, civil rights affirming, rat-a-tat-tatty, secretive, overlicking the envelope, Kosher salty, Palance-faced, dead balloon, a tad sausage-casing-like, like a Thrift Store crutch, the Jesus nail hole (as a compliment), alpha-loaf, dumpster rent, too Jewy, Ryan or Rian or Ryen, chemically induced boner, horseradish, taint zit, reverse cow skrunk, 3-up-3 down, urgently unnecessary, Chinese labored, viscous, adult diaper, gravy spittoon, Rock-free, Curbside appliance.

Temptation

510 The word in the term "statutory rape" that judges focus on is not "statutory."

511 Since your girlfriend is not in the band, she is not entitled to the same hospitality (i.e., free drinks, all access) as you. However, if she's hot, make her the cowbell player and she's in.

512 Your girlfriend never cares about the band, she only cares about who is at the show. If she cares about the band, she wants to dump you and date the lead singer.

513 Trying to sleep with a fan's girlfriend is bad karma.

514 Panties larger than a size 8 that are tossed onstage should be set on fire.

The Wisdom of the Cell Phone

515 Concerning your cell-phone plan, be sure all your friends and family have the same provider so you can get one of those free-on-the-same-network plans. Your girl/boyfriend and parents may drive you crazy, but at least it will be free.

516 Making long-distance phone calls to home from a pay phone where the only words you partially understand are "phone calls cheap" will rapidly deplete your savings.

The Psalm of Law Enforcement

517 Border patrols really will strip-search you. So be nice.

518 If you get pulled over on tour by the cops, pretend you're a Christian rock band on its way to play a revival. Chances are the cop is a brain-dead Christian who will let you off the hook to spread the good word. As soon as he's gone, bust out and blaze.

Golden Rules

519 If you're in one of those bands with a message, odds are nobody came to see you or to hear your pampered ass talk about the world's injustices. Please do everyone a favor and buy an LED sign and scroll your message at the bottom, like the nightly news.

520 If you're under the drinking age and a club employee asks for your ID, the proper response is not "I'm playing tonight." The law is "You Must Be 21," not "21 or in a Band."

521 Never pass up a free meal.

522 In an effort to psych everybody in the band, tape this sign somewhere on an amp or a drum head: "PMA (greater than or equal to) AKG (Another Killer Gig)."

523 If you're making any decent money on the road, routinely send it home in the form of money orders. God knows what your bone-headed tour manager will do. Actually, God does know what he'll do; he'll either lose it or blow it on nose candy.

524 Always remember: Duct tape is a touring musician's best friend.

525 If your band gets an offer to play on a cruise ship or an extended stay in a hotel in Asia, things are winding down.

526 Be aware that it is not the job of paying customers to "get the message of the song."

527 Touring the Midwest during the winter is always a horrible idea.

528 The man with the black Sharpie is always king.

529 It's never wise to have a four-band bill on a weekday.

530 If you're playing LA, have insulting business cards made to hand to the legion of industry scum who introduce themselves with theirs first as they ask for free merchandise.

531 There is no better way to be an ugly American than to be impressed by fast-food restaurants overseas.

532 Everybody at every show is either in another band or dating someone in another band. That means nobody's there to see your band. They're there to be seen, to look like they're giving you support, and to promote themselves.

533 Never trust anyone wearing two different bands' merchandise at the same time.

The Psalm of the Album, Song & Studio

534 Any record that runs over the 45-minute mark is considered a double album and must be judged by double-album criteria. You're making a statement by doing this. Does your record slip neatly between classic double albums? No? Then edit it.

535 Any band that feels the need to indulge itself with a concept album should consider that no one wants to hear an album's worth of tracks referring to mythical warriors, mutant dragons, or a great journey across the cosmos.

536 Composing "rock symphonies" is a contradiction in terms.

537 Releasing your demos later only acknowledges that you had it right the first time.

538 For a band that has been around fewer than five years or a band that has fewer than three albums, it is impossible to have a masterpiece.

539 There are few albums that will ever be considered masterpieces. Don't be even remotely shocked that yours isn't one of them.

The Wisdom of the Album Title

540 No self-titled albums unless it is your first record. Don't be an ass. You blew your chance.

541 Album titles should never contain the words "movement," "suite," "opus," "concept," "part," or any roman numerals.

542 It is never appropriate to title your album with a bunch of words that have no association to one another and do not make a complete phrase or sentence.

543 Never thank Jesus in the credits.

544 Reconsider thanking every band that you've ever performed with. This is especially the case with the two or three "big bands" you've shared a stage with because, more than likely, they didn't have a choice in having you open, couldn't care less how many people you draw in your own hometown, and probably didn't even see you play.

545 Inside jokes in the thank-you list are strictly forbidden.

546 Album titles with conflicting terms such as *Nobody Knows This Is Everywhere*, *Building Something Out of Nothing*, *Ancient Melodies of the Future*, etc., are not intriguing, beguiling, or amusing. They are dumb.

547 No symbols. It's a title, not graffiti.

548 If your album title is a sentence or longer, expect everyone to shorten it in the most unflattering way possible.

The Wisdom of the Album Cover

549 If you decide to issue your LP in a gatefold sleeve, make sure you make good use of the space. A gatefold sleeve is no place for minimalism.

550 Never give each band member his own thank-you section in the liner notes. All the people you thank will hate you in two years.

551 For record covers or promotional merchandise, hire a professional to design it. If you can't afford it, leave it blank.

552 References to robots, cover art with robots, and robotic themes are all tired and prove that you are completely lacking in good aesthetic judgment.

553 Reconsider doing a 10-inch record. They look like toy records and they don't file correctly.

554 Never put a sticker on the front of your album stating "featuring the hit singles . . . " The album just came out and couldn't possibly have spawned a hit single yet.

555 With rare exception, album covers with animals have never been cool.

The Book of the Good Word

556 Popular bands have B-sides. Unpopular bands just have "other songs."

557 A CD burned on your mom's computer is not a "release."

558 A CD that your parents paid for is not a "release."

559 You are not a "musician," you are "in a band."

560 Rare records rarely, if ever, equate to "good" records.

561 If a song falls below 78 beats per minute, it's considered a dirge. If it falls below 78 beats per minute and has a steel guitar or Dobro, it's considered country.

562 Musicians that describe themselves as singer/songwriters are never equally competent at both.

The Book of Album Reviews

563 If you're going to poison the world with yet another horrible album and send it out for review, at least make it obvious which is your band's name and which is the name of the album.

564 If an album is described as having "layers of emotion," that simply means it contains some mediocre rockers but is mostly just an apologetic excuse for having a couple of sappy, sad-sack ballads.

565 If an album is described as having an "unswerving sense of purpose," it means that it is a self-important, holier-than-thou piece of tired, regurgitated cud that has only one song played in ten barely noticeably different ways.

566 If your band has been credited for "saving rock and roll," then save every last dime you make on your one successful tour. You'll need the money later.

567 Online reviews of your record do not count.

568 Under no circumstances should you ever play your band's CD or demo for someone unless they specifically ask to hear it. Don't ask or tell them to listen to it. Putting them on the spot to provide feedback is rude.

569 To describe your album with hyperbole and then follow it with the "fact" that said hyperbole is an understatement (example: "To say this record was a monumental effort would be an understatement.") is the weakest of one-sheet bio writing, and the author's fingers should quickly be run through a paper shredder.

570 Always refer to your band's upcoming album as "the best work we've ever done," no matter how awful it really is.

The Wisdom of Records

571 No matter how low you try to set the price, your record will still be overpriced.

572 Overpriced CDs should come with fancy packaging and a special bonus disc to justify the extra cost.

573 Having a limited pressing of a release ensures that everybody will buy the record not for the music but for the investment potential.

The Book of Song Titles

574 Use extreme caution putting "Rock & Roll" in the title of a song. It had better really rock, which means you can't use the phrase for a ballad.

575 Unless you're a hardcore punk or ska band, you can never have a song named after the band itself.

Hymns & Lyrics

576 Never write a song that complains about how your previous record didn't sell nearly as well as you hoped.

577 Any mention of wizards, unicorns, or spacecraft in a song automatically puts you in the prog genre, which, in turn, means that you owe somebody your lunch money.

578 If you can't hum the melody to a song you wrote, it has too many notes.

579 If you write a song about having sex with a family member, it must be set up north, as setting it in Alabama or, God forbid, Mississippi, is just too easy.

580 All great rock songs are about women, beer, or the lack of either. If you write a song about anything else, at least find a way to make it funny.

581 Any kind of songwriting about the record industry, nuclear war, or pedophilia should only be described as "black comedy."

582 Using the word "buggery" is always funny, but there are extra points if it can rhyme.

Writing the Good Word

583 If the drummer writes the majority of the songs, it means your band is filled with mediocre songwriters.

584 Acid casualties always write their best songs while on acid.

585 If you can steal a great band's riffs and get away with it, you can stop writing your own.

586 Great songs are never born out of "jamming."

587 Never let a drummer write a song or do anything other than drum. Ever.

588 If you did not help write the songs, do not expect an equal cut of the royalties.

The Parable of the Girl Who Misheard Lyrics Yet Still Insisted on Giving Voice to Song

For it came to pass, in a house of pre-collegiate learning, there strode a girl. And the girl possessed the beauty of a birch tree's wind-loosed blossoms, falling to earth in autumn twilight—but still not in a way that one would deem her beyond reach, and so she had many suitors.

But none of them tarried long, for she housed a minor devil. The devil did not make her bark in the moonlight, or spew grub-worms from her mouth, or cause her monthly cursedness to issue forth as crows.

No, for this eldritch soul-pirate caused in her a burning love of popular music, a love that fogged, flickered, and flummoxed the steady flame of logic, so that in her excitement she'd sing along with whatever tune flitted about in the immediate air.

And what she'd sing would not be the song as the artist intended. It was whatever her first impression was of that song's lyrics. Thus, a lover who was, say, trapped in a car on a lengthy journey would have to hear, "Mices wear faces, you're addicted to love," or "Hey, Mr. Tangerine Man" and "Joy to the bitches in the cheap blue jeans."

And soon they would depart.

I mean, "Mices wear faces"? Come on.

589 Never write a song that talks about the Internet.

590 Writing a great song is one hundred times harder than soloing all over the place or writing "complex" compositions—and one hundred times more pleasurable to listen to.

591 Every time you write a song about Jesus, another natural disaster happens somewhere in the world.

592 All of the tunings, noise, and riffs that you believe to be original are not. There's absolutely nothing new you can do with a guitar at this stage in rock's evolution.

593 If you can't hum the melody to a song you wrote, it has too many notes.

The Wisdom of Song Augmentation

594 No song can be markedly improved with the use of rhythmic hand claps or finger snaps.

595 Never have fake sex sounds, like heavy breathing, in a song. It sounds like you just ate a huge party sub and were forced to run around your house twice.

The Golden Rule of Song Length

596 Unless the song has multiple references to a mystic sword or dragons, keep it under five minutes.

The Psalm of the Producer

597 Nobody with a shred of taste has ever bought an album because a certain someone produced it. Don't brag about your producer.

598 If you are one of the few decent, mindful, and cool musicians on the planet, don't waste your time trying to small talk with the engineer or producer. They're almost always certifiably insane.

599 Studio engineers have bad taste. In everything.

600 Don't let the recording engineer talk you into using one of the amps in the studio that he is accustomed to recording. It makes things easier for him, but your studio time isn't about him. It's about your "art."

601 Never record at a studio where the main engineer wears flip-flops with dark socks.

602 Never record at a studio where the engineer has his children or cats running around the control room. You're recording your album, not running a day-care facility.

603 To keep an engineer happy, you must make sure you feed him.

604 If you don't laugh at the studio engineer's "jokes," he will ruin your album.

605 Don't let a drug addict be the recording engineer because he or

she may discover much later that the mic fell out of the kick drum.

606 Don't overdub your solos with sweet little riffs. The engineer and your band are sitting in the playback room laughing at you.

607 Don't tell people that your album was recorded by a hot engineer if you're lame enough to think that it's going to afford you any credibility.

608 If you extol the virtues of recording exclusively to tape, you better know what the hell you are talking about.

609 There is such thing as a guitar tone having too much distortion in the studio.

610 Describing vocal harmonies as being "sun drenched" just means a band stacked multiple layers of vocals together in a studio that they could never pull off live. It also means, at this late stage of the game, that you still find merit in ripping off the Beach Boys.

611 If you want your music to sound sourly out of tune and completely dated, use a Mellotron.

612 "Lo-fi" really means you "couldn't afford to record in a real studio."

613 If you are going to have backward masking in your recording, it absolutely must be because your band is satanic.

The Wisdom of Takes

614 Remember, everyone is looking at you. Don't screw up, because if you do, you're costing the band a lot of money.

615 There is no such thing as a "one-take wonder."

616 Play every song like you invented it.

The Book of Mixing & Dubbing

617 Never mix a song to sound great for television. Your video, at best, will be downloaded as a substandard file on the Internet.

618 Don't complain to the engineer that the guitar isn't loud enough when he is tracking vocals and you're not the vocalist.

619 No overdubbing two drum sets or drum takes by a single drummer. It always sounds like a bag of puppies being thrown down the stairs.

The Book of Sound Augmentation

620 If you've just mastered how to play a barre chord, some may wonder how you got an entire orchestra to play on your hit single.

621 Recording with an uncommon instrument is never uncommon.

622 Using a xylophone during quiet passages to "add accents" will only make you look like you have a passing interest in jazz.

623 Don't let your hired horn players polish off the liquor and drugs until after they've laid down all their tracks.

Golden Rules of the Studio

624 Your dog does not belong at the studio. Nor do your friends.

625 Never bring a "posse" into the studio. Only the band, engineers, and one non–band member are allowed. Having a crowd in the studio only ensures that you'll try to figure out how to work them all in, thus creating really bad hand claps or shout-outs during any given song.

626 Don't touch the console unless you're the engineer, mixer, or producer.

627 Taking interesting notes and pictures only shows you care more about yourself than actually making a good record. If you feel it is necessary to have pictures of the band while in the studio, hire a professional.

628 If anyone passes out in the studio control room, it's open season for teabagging.

629 Don't smoke in the studio. Instead, vaporize.

630 If you bring snacks to the studio, bring enough to share.

631 If your guitar isn't set up, it has no business being recorded.

632 If you break wind in an isolation booth, give a courtesy shout and tell someone before they open the door. There is nowhere for that foul air to go except out the door once it's opened.

633 Never let your bandmates have a farting contest on the control room couch that one of you will be spending the night on.

634 Never personally master your own recordings unless you really don't want anyone to listen to them.

635 When you get a copy of your recording from the studio and it sounds horrible, before you blame the engineer, you should first ponder whether your music is horrible.

The Book of Bad Ideas

636 If you hire a famous hip-hop artist to come in and drop beats and remix a song, chances are it's not going to save your already mediocre release.

637 Never smoke before you do your vocals unless you intentionally want it to sound terrible.

638 The integrity of your recording may ultimately suffer if your heroin-to-blood ratio exceeds your signal-to-noise ratio.

639 Don't sleep with the studio interns who get your food for you.

N the sixth day, God said, "Let there be lesser creatures who they themselves want to be musicians." God made these creatures according to their utility: guitar, drum, and bass techs; house engineer; monitor engineer; light guy; and tour manager. God made these primarily, according to their kind, to score drugs for the band. And there was a mag light and there was a Leatherman, then there was a smell, and then there was a laminate, and then there was a lousy, falsely authoritative attitude about who was allowed on the bus and other such things, and then there were old crew people who regaled (bored) younger people with tales of how they roadie'd a Starz/Blue Oyster Cult tour in 1980 and witnessed a food fight at a hotel pool, and so on, and so on.

The Psalm of the Crew

1 If it's green, smoke it. If it moves, fuck it. If it doesn't move, put it in the van.

2 Even if he can't play his way out of a paper bag, always have one guy on tour who can successfully back up the trailer.

3 You are not a legitimate band playing actual music until at least one member of your crew has a one-word, one-syllable name like "Tank," "Brick," "Horse," or "Meat" and has acquired this nickname by doing something really stupid.

4 Being part of the road crew means that you're probably really good at playing video games (among other mind-numbing habits). The band will want you to teach them the ins and outs of certain games as they while away time on the bus. This talent will probably result in a stupid nickname (see verse 3, above).

5 Acceptable previous employment for roadies includes newspaper carrier, pocket fisherman, and off-season lobster poacher. Those jobs are actually much more interesting than being a band's lap dog. Acceptable post-roadie employment is limited to drug counselor (only after rehab), porn star, co-author of a rock memoir that won't get published, and guy who sits around boring other people with stories.

6 It's a proven fact that people working at clubs, especially in a technical context, are dirtbags with some sort of criminal record. As such, they probably have great stories.

7 "Local crew" is regional slang for "personal slave."

Idle Hands Are the Devil's Playground

8 Before going on the road for the next ten years with a band you don't like, consider a career as a hobo.

9 In the future, after you've ruined your back and pooped out your liver due to drinking, it's possible that you'll be interviewed for an oral history of the band with which you worked. When that happens, it's important to remember that you are not a writer.

10 After ten years on the road with any band, you'll undoubtedly say, "I really should've gone to college instead."

11 If the band you're working for isn't playing for more than 300 people, your presence is largely unnecessary.

12 If you do, in fact, have a great talent for accounting and keeping track of inventory, consider working at a bank or a warehouse. Your management skills will most certainly be better recognized and rewarded.

13 There are a dozen trained chimps that can take your place. Don't stop to think about it, just keep humping the gear.

14 If the band you're working for can't remember your name, it's because they've got more important things to worry about, like writing songs and performing live every night.

15 Don't get bummed when you have to pay for drinks. If you were that valuable to the band's existence, they'd be big enough to have a separate tour rider just for you guys.

Sins of the Flesh

16 Despite the popular long-running joke, there is not a rational woman on the planet who will sleep with a roadie.

17 The only acceptable place for road crew to have sex with groupies is inside road cases.

18 If you get some action after the show, it's not because you're hot, it's because you work for a band whose members she/he wants to sleep with.

The Wisdom of the Guitar Tech

19 "Guitar techs" are basically guitar players who are too stoned or drunk to keep their own bands together.

20 Crouching behind a guitar amp during the show does not immediately inform the crowd that you're needed on stage. In fact, it's probably your unconscious attempt at showing how self-important you really aren't.

Seeing the Light

21 Light techs should remember

that the crowd never goes home humming the lights.

22 The difference between a sound guy and a light tech is that a sound guy can do lights.

23 The sound crew should realize that nobody in the audience started the evening by saying, "I'm going to go hear a band tonight."

24 Without a sound guy, it's radio. Without a light tech, it's a Christmas tree.

The Wisdom of the Sound Guy

25 If the sound guy has a ponytail, everybody knows what it's covering up.

26 If you're playing a small club, there is never a need for you to use a flashlight to clear a path through the crowd to move your equipment.

27 Unless you're the sound guy at the show, leave your flashlight and Leatherman at home.

28 Just tell a band to turn it up or turn it down. When you start rattling on about how many dBs the band is pushing, they just tune out and learn to hate you. Keep it simple.

29 When in doubt, and on tour,

the house sound guy is the man to ask for narcotics.

30 Everybody thinks they're funny. Most people aren't, especially sound men.

31 "Sound man" does not mean "DJ." You are not entitled to talk to the audience through the PA.

32 If you see a smiley-faced EQ on the mixing desk in front of you, lay off the amphetamines.

33 Most sound men should have their ponytails clipped off and fed to them.

34 If you have to duct-tape your mics or mic stands to keep them from falling apart, then you need to spend less on PBR and more on your equipment.

35 The band doesn't want to be your friend. The fans don't want to be your friend. The club owner doesn't want to be your friend. They all just want you to go easier on the treble.

36 All sound guys are, without exception, failed musicians who hate the band's existence. They usually have out-of-date taste in music and are just waiting to ruin their sound.

Recommended Phrases to Say to a Not-So-Great Band as They Come Off Stage

Many Good Guys are in many Bad Bands, which has led to the acronym GGBB. In light of this, when a band is stepping off their hallowed pulpit from either a sparse room of attendees or a full house of screaming fans, try to evasively compliment anything. The light show. Their merchandise. Anything. When you're desperate, try muttering one of the following phrases to escape from a potentially awkward situation.

"The audience seemed really attentive."

"Your bass player was really holding it down."

"You guys just will not compromise."

"Hey, what label puts out your records?"

"Your drummer looked like a hurricane of squirrels."

"Man, you guys looked like you were having so much fun!"

"It's nice to hear a drummer who really knows how to put some step into the kick drum."

"It takes guts to get up onstage and do what you do."

"You can tell you guys listen to really good music."

"I've never heard anything like that before."

"Was that last song a cover?"

"We had to straighten out our beer situation with the bar manager, but it sounded great backstage."

"I saw loads of people really digging it!"

"Your merch looked bad ass, I caught some chicks checking out the table."

"Hey, let's go do shots!"

AND on the seventh day, God had finished the work he had been doing, so he rested from all his toil . . . until a fan wanted him to sign something. And God signed it, but the fan also wanted a photo, and God took a photo with the fan, but the fan wanted God to sing happy birthday to a friend over a cell phone, and God sang happy birthday, and then the fan and the fan's friends resembled that animal that God had become so familiar with . . . the sheep. And then there became far more fans than there was rock and roll, and the fans dressed a particular way, and the fans all thought the same way, and sometimes the fans were indistinguishable from the rock and roll bands, and then God considered some form of natural genocide, but God was unsure of how to get all these idiots in one place without wiping out some actual decent people, so God gave up on the genocide idea and instead placed a lot of faith in drug overdoses and aging, and so on, and so on.

The Book of the Live Show

1 If you're supposed to be on the list but aren't, you aren't important enough to insult every staff member in the club because of it.

2 If you're exceedingly tall and the room's packed, stand at the back of the room.

3 While standing in front of a band that does not play metal, those that throw devil horns shall have the offending appendage removed and subsequently forced down their throats.

4 When the drummer breaks a stick and throws it into the crowd and it hits you on the head, you have first dibs. Also, don't save things like that. Go to a store and buy a drumstick if you really want one.

5 If the band killed it, don't just clap. Give them a real hand and help load out their equipment.

6 If you ever use a cell phone instead of a lighter during a ballad, it's time to start smoking again.

7 If a mic gets knocked over, you are allowed to set it back up. However, that doesn't allow you a discount on band merchandise after the show.

8 While in the audience, you can never leave a jacket or purse on stage while the band is playing. It is a stage, not a coat check.

9 Every show has the crazy dancing dude that creeps out and amuses the crowd. If you ever find yourself as that dude, don't be surprised if you don't have any friends.

10 If your friend isn't at a show

with you, he or she didn't care enough to buy a ticket. Calling him or her during the show and then holding up the phone so he or she can hear a distorted representation of what the band is playing isn't helping anybody.

11 Never start a drum circle after a show in the camping area of a music festival.

12 Unless a show is in a church or a coffee house and the band requires no amplification, sitting on the floor is strictly prohibited. Not only are most floors absolutely filthy, but chances are you'll get your hand stepped on or, at worst, be trampled during a stampede.

13 If you are invited to watch a friend's band play, you are allowed to leave after ten minutes if they suck. Points are never scored for enduring a horrible performance.

14 Never walk across the stage. If you do, you're just showing that you're confused about where catering is.

15 If a band has inflatable stage props, it is the audience's responsibility to try to pop them.

16 No matter how crowded a show might be, it's never a good idea to urinate anywhere but the bathroom.

17 Don't urinate on people's feet.

18 Unless it's just you in the audience, you're sadly mistaken if you think someone in the band just made eye contact with you.

19 Many bands you enjoy are just simply not very good live. Unlike musical taste, this point is not subjective. Also, bands with poorly recorded albums will most likely be just as horrible when you pay to see them.

20 Never go to a band's concert if their T-shirt costs more than a ticket to the show.

21 Never pay an excessive amount to see a concert unless the band is scheduled to bring dead members back to life during the performance.

22 Do not sing along with a band at a show unless you are absolutely sure of the words.

23 Never take the band's set list unless you plan on selling it later.

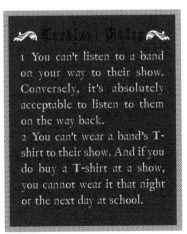

🎵 **Cardinal Rules** 🎵

1 You can't listen to a band on your way to their show. Conversely, it's absolutely acceptable to listen to them on the way back.

2 You can't wear a band's T-shirt to their show. And if you do buy a T-shirt at a show, you cannot wear it that night or the next day at school.

24 For every beer you steal from the band, an angel loses its wings.

The Golden Rules of Heckling

25 Don't ever tell people to shut up at a show. Conversely, if you are on stage and have a microphone and an amplified instrument going through a PA, and you can't make more interesting noise than an office dweller with a can of beer, you are in trouble.

26 Never sing aloud along with the songs unless you can do it in key and at a volume that only you can hear. In any other situation, no one will appreciate your contribution.

27 Don't get upset when your heckle gets returned to you in a much funnier and degrading manner. Granted, most bands can't handle anything less than pure adoration from the audience, but there are a few sharp people playing music who have no problem letting you know that you are a talentless, drunk idiot whose lineage may contain canine DNA.

28 Never yell "Free Bird" to a band. If you are in a band that has "Free Bird" yelled to it, know the song well enough to give a torturous twenty-minute rendition.

29 Never yell out for a band to play their most obscure song. It isn't on the set list because they don't like playing it.

30 If a band has a female member, it is absurdly imperative that there's a guy in the crowd to yell "Take it off!" after every song.

31 If you can't think of anything more interesting to shout at your favorite artist on stage than "We love you," at least have the fortitude to back it up by proving it after the show.

Good Will Toward All Musicians

32 Moshing at a show has gone the way of "The Wave" at sporting events. It's easy to get caught up in the moment when you're there, but to everyone else watching and not participating, you're a jackass.

33 Pretend that the stage is the band's office and that people can enter only if they work there. You, most certainly, do not.

34 If you go to shows where the main activity is moshing, you have strong homoerotic tendencies.

35 While in the audience, never offer the band a beer, a cigarette, or a light. It's akin to feeding the bears.

36 Never do spirit fingers within inches of the lead guitar player. It will not improve the guitarist's abil-

ity, but it will improve your ability to look like an asshole.

Golden Rules of Conversing with the Band

37 If you think you're sounding stupid, you're exactly a half hour behind everybody else. Apologize and leave immediately. The band has the rest of the night to talk about how much of a jackass you are.

38 Saying "you guys sounded tight" or "you had great energy" to a band after they're done playing is a polite way of getting the point across that you think they are a lousy band.

39 If you're interacting with the band after the show, refrain from telling members how much their music means to you. In the band's eyes, it changes you from fan to stalker in the time it takes to say the words.

40 If you're a dude, remember that the members of the band didn't get into music to meet other dudes. Stay away so the ladies can climb aboard the bus.

41 Never ever strike up a conversation with the drummer.

42 Either ask the band beforehand if it's okay to record their show or just don't ask them at all. Letting them know afterward that you did so without permission puts you in a dangerous position with moody

musicians who are worried about their inconsistent, and occasionally weak, performances.

43 "You rock!" is not a sincere compliment to any band.

44 Never take the band's last drink.

45 Upon meeting a musician you idolize, don't say: "I'm a really big fan." And for God's sake, don't ask for an autograph. Offering to get free drugs or inquiring about the after-party is acceptable.

The Seven Commandments of Appearance

46 Know ahead of time that getting a band tattoo is a perfect way to show people what you used to listen to before your twentieth birthday.

47 "CBGB" T-shirts are never a good indication that you are "hip to the scene."

48 If you have a "Death to False Metal" tattoo anywhere on your body, you must someday reimburse your parents for buying it for you.

49 If there's a patch on your jacket or shirt that's not your name, you must force your girlfriend to buy you some new clothes.

50 Anyone who wishes to buy any Ramones-related merchandise must be able to name all members of the

original lineup and a minimum of five of their songs.

51 Never purchase a vintage, overpriced T-shirt that wasn't your idea at the time. Everyone who sees you wearing it knows you paid too much for it.

52 Wearing a muscle shirt and not actually having any muscles is one reason why the underage girls at the show don't want to sleep with you. You shouldn't be flirting with pre-teen girls anyway, you pedophile.

The Psalm of the Groupie

53 Even the hottest groupies usually have to work their way through the road crew before finally getting to the band. Keep your chin up and your kneepads on. Your time is coming.

54 Do not expect to make friends with a roadie in the hopes that he will take you on tour unless you smoke him out, buy him lots of good beer, provide him with girls, or all of the above.

55 If you're ever offered a backstage pass left over from "the Tulsa show," be aware that if you take it, you'll be in a sexually humiliating scenario by the night's end.

56 If you're dating a member of a band, you're a groupie. Stop trying to act like you're somehow a notch above a groupie. You're not a rock

star by default. You're a groupie.

57 If you want your band to break up, sleep with the singer's current girlfriend or ex-girlfriend about whom all the songs are written.

58 If you are the girlfriend of a band member and you attend band practice, you will be referred to as "Yoko."

The Golden Rules of the Pickup

59 If you feel the need to constantly protect your girlfriend at a show, perhaps it's best that she make other plans.

60 Stop trying to pick up people of the opposite sex in the front row of a show while a band is playing. Your feeble attempts at getting action will only be hindered by having to scream everything into your poor victim's ear, especially when your pickup lines entail name-dropping every mediocre artist to come out of your pathetic town.

61 If you're a woman and you're at a show, act like every guy there is a creepy rapist unless he's somebody famous who might also have cocaine. This is called "Feminism in Rock."

62 Gentlemen, if you go to concerts by sensitive singer/songwriter types to show how equally sensitive you are to ladies, chances are you've never seen, let alone touched, a naked person of the opposite sex.

Recognizing Boundaries with Prophets

63 Any and all stash you carry onto the bus is now community property, so fork it over.

64 If you're invited onto the band's bus, don't sit down if there's room to stand.

65 Never ask the band for a ride anywhere.

66 When the bus driver gets on the bus, you get off the bus.

Let There Be Rest

67 If a band stays at your house and you have a practice space or studio setup, don't try to talk the band into jamming with you. They just want to sleep, get drunk, or take a shower, not go for a noodle-fest with some sycophantic dweeb. Keep it in the case.

68 If you're hospitable enough to have a band stay at your house, don't do so thinking it will just be one big booze-soaked, drug-addled party. You're only saving the band the expense of a hotel room. Let them sleep.

69 A hot meal will win the hearts of a band on tour more than almost anything. Additionally, if you want said band to listen to your demo, consider baking it into something.

The Psalm of the Fanboy

70 Fans that dress like the band are just asking to be pummeled. If you want to be in the band that badly, you might as well bring your gear to the show and play along from the audience.

71 No waiting to get an autograph for more than half an hour (although even that seems a bit too long). The band is either getting high or already back at the hotel.

72 If you ask a crew member for a guitar pick or set list, it's best to listen to the first answer you get. Any subsequent requests will be met with an increasing insult and chance of removal from the venue.

73 Showing up at a show three hours early to get a primo space in front of the stage is reaffirming to all those around you that you don't have a life.

74 Only bands that are older than the average record store employee are allowed to be discussed as having "seminal work."

75 Carrying an amplifier does not grant you "with the band" status.

76 If you can name your favorite band with one answer, you're not a fan. You're in a cult.

77 Don't attempt to reveal how much of a guitar nerd you are by showing how interested you are in the guitar player's pedals.

78 Don't assume you're a friend to the band. Unless you set proper boundaries, the band will eventually turn against you.

79 It's not just creepy if you love a band enough to camp out alongside their bus for an entire afternoon. It's really creepy.

80 Shut up about the fact that you used to be in a band.

The Psalm of the Record Nerd

81 Colored vinyl never sounds better. In fact, white vinyl is so poor that the record might as well be pressed into cotton candy.

82 When asked what kind of music you enjoy, it's not acceptable to reply that you like all kinds of music.

83 You found that copy of [insert band name here] CD in the bargain bin for a reason. Don't use nostalgia to cover up the fact that you have lousy taste in music.

84 Never ask how many records somebody owns.

85 Never refer to the amount of music you own in "bytes" or "gigs."

86 Don't impress people with how obscure or enormous your record collection is. Ultimately, it isn't either.

87 Don't just tell friends about your favorite band's album; give them your copy. Now you have an excuse to buy another good album.

88 Someone who collects "white label" advance-copy records is always a white kid who listens exclusively to black music who should also be forced to drink multiple bottles of Wite-Out.

The Wisdom of the Camera

89 Stop filming the band with your cell phone while they're on stage. The fidelity and picture will be utterly substandard. Try enjoying the moment for once.

90 Just because your phone has a camera doesn't mean you need to use it repeatedly during the show. Nobody needs to reminisce immediately. Taking dozens of low-quality snapshots only serves to draw attention to the fact that you're into being a low-budget journalist instead of someone who paid to enjoy a performance.

91 Every artist lacking artistic talent is a photographer. They're trendy and the easiest to find in a crowd.

Critics & Other Heathens

92 When interviewing a band, let the musician talk. Don't let it be a platform for you to impress them or, worse yet, impress those for whom the interview is intended.

93 Don't ever use the adjectives "swirling" or "effervescent" unless talking about a toilet and a soda drink, respectively.

94 If, as a writer, the best you've got is "it sounds like band X crossed with band Y," you're not a writer. You're a cliché.

95 Just because you wrote a review for a local publication doesn't mean you automatically get into the band's show for free.

96 Critics who say that a band sounds like "[another band] on [a drug]" must have done the drug in question. It's a simple question of credibility.

97 The term "seminal" for the purposes of rock criticism is completely obsolete.

98 If you write a music review like it's a recipe, you're not a writer. You're a chef.

99 Your "great" work will always be forgotten once the next issue is out.

100 Music editors are not frustrated musicians; they are fans who have cleverly figured out how to get free records.

101 Music writers aren't just failed musicians; they're also failed writers.

102 Music journalists who identify themselves as being from any publication must immediately follow it up by saying, "and you don't owe me anything."

The Book of Graphic Design

103 Under no circumstances should you ever do a record cover (or any work) for a hippie band. No self-respecting musicians will ever hire you after that. (Actually, no one with any self-respect, not just musicians).

104 No design gets better with some old 1950s picture of some unexplained person on it. This is a cop-out and an admission that you just couldn't think of anything else to do. Leave it blank or, better yet, hire a professional.

105 Never let somebody in the band design the band's artwork.

106 The amount you'll get paid for a project is inversely proportional to how rewarding the project actually is.

107 Just because you're working for a cool label doesn't mean you won't be ripped off. As is often the case, their swank offices are paid for through the art of ripping people off.

108 If your clever band T-shirt

concept is to steal the logo of a famous band, pick a great logo from a great band.

109 It's never wise to presume that a band and their label will agree on the simple concept that you'll get paid for your work.

110 It's best to assume that you'll never get paid, never get thanked, and never get credited.

111 Don't put anything other than the band's name on their stickers. It's all useless information that nobody cares about.

112 Don't let bands talk you into being their design slave. If they already have the record designed in their heads, you'll end up with something you won't want to put in your portfolio. It won't reflect your style or sensibility, and in the long run it'll hurt your career.

113 You should always be open to band's ideas and suggestions. After all, they are artists and creative people, too. Just be sure not to let them take control of what should be your own design.

114 If you don't want to design posters, don't put posters in your portfolio.

Worshipping False Prophets

115 If you're a promoter, don't give the band some full-color copies of a poster you designed like it's some big deal. You're a failed designer and everybody knows it.

116 Promoting shows can be done by any shallow, money-grubbing clown with a passing knowledge of contemporary music. It's why most choose this vapid profession in the first place.

117 Behind publicists, promoters are the most loathed and least thanked or trusted people in the music industry.

118 Do not assume that the "girl with the band" asking about drink tickets or the guarantee is "just a band member's girlfriend." She may be in the band, and may even be the one who actually started the band and booked the show.

119 If the posters weren't screen-printed, they're worthless.

The Parable of the Critic Who Always Felt Betrayed

And lo, there came upon the land a music critic, who so loved and protected the new, and the unsung, that for them to be sung, even by the lowest pressgangs and whisperers on the Earth, would cause him to scorn and loathe that which he once elevated.

And yea his sickness grew in him till he could no longer bear even the dimmest light of recognition of praise to warm the brows of those who toiled in the darkness. And see him now—a gibbering, stubble-chinned half-a-man, communicating to the three subscribers of his podcast, shouting to the ether his credo, "And it is at the moment a band constructs the bare skeleton of a memorable melody that I am OVER THEM."

And he is forever in love with disgust.

AND so the great rock prophet did set out to glimpse the yielding of his precious countenance through many a wise oracle of forgotten rock recordings and failed attempts at stardom and saw maddening disinterest in his plight to save the world of rock from utter folly. Neither the meat-headed banger nor the methodical noodler saw fit to heed the admissions of those gone before them and many a false prophet and warner-monger did usher in the very end of rock. And, yea, the prophet beheld the ten heralds of the Arockalypse and with narrow vision did name these beasts and foretold their wrath:

SXCMJ3000

Originally designed as a random sentence generator, the SXCMJ3000 eventually found use by certain evil forces and false prophets as a device for randomly generating rock lyrics, rock songs, and rock band names. Through a series of free downloadable updates, the computer began to "learn" how to book bands on a national tour, sign bands and make money off them, and, in the end, magically discover how to invent them wholly and charge them with an amazing energy called "buzz" in a fashion identical to the humans it replaced. This would confuse the masses of rock bands who believed that anyone could be a rock star because the creations of the machine seemed to come out of nowhere and, although they were no different than all the other bands, they seemed to get more attention than a juggling vagina act from YouTuberius.

YouTuberius

Thought at one time to be an oracle of great wonder and promise, the false idol did quickly show his true nature to the rock prophet when his music video of the week with fourteen million hits was a SXCMJ computation misusing a running machine as a gay Busby Berkeley jungle gym.

The Myspacebook of Oblivion

The prophet saw a teeming wasteland of bands alphabetized, numbered, and categorized by such meaningless tags as postcore, grindjazz, and Christian slamwave. The simple slaves were given to the constant invitation of friend and fellowship to the unknown and disinterested masses, paying exorbitant prices for the machinery with which to ask this easily self-answered question to as many as one thousand people in a single day and, yea, verily even to annoy those parties dumb enough to take council by postering their site with flyers for shows that may not even be in the same country and videos of the last dorm room they practiced in. This yawning chasm of useless information so clouded the vision of rocker near and far that their plight would end in them sending the same friend request to one thousand bands a day and having 240,000 friends and absolutely no fans whatsoever.

The Buddyheaded Pitchforkagon

And verily as the prophet did stumble away from the Myspacebook of Oblivion did he find himself staring into the eyes of the great Pitchforkagon, a massive bloated animal with a seemingly nice head but a tongue of many forks that did battle with many a decent but not brilliant rock band, taking their money and spirit for advertising and free mp3s and leaving their dying corpse on a pile of names on the side of the page for three months before striking it from the record forever. Some rockers whose fight was bold were relegated to tales not longer than a paragraph on one of the links under the heading "Features." The false prophets the

Pitchforkagon confessed as brilliant were actually computations from the mighty SXCMJ3000.

CDBabylazon.com

In the great time of vinyl, a young lover of rock would go to market at the local record store, where each new discovery could mean certain wonder or a saddening waste of hard-earned cash. This trade, however, made the value of the good recording quite high, and those records known to be good were anticipated with much unrest and in high esteem. Making these recordings was laborious and costly and only those who were convinced they were worthy would bother to pony up without major label money or a trust fund. In later times, the information super highway led to a new market where recordings made on a whim might be bought and sold without leaving the dank of one's own lair. What came from this new market of trinket sounds was a gaping maw of home-produced tool knock-offs that would ultimately make finding a gem almost as impossible as finding a drummer in L.A. without a coke habit who will practice for free.

Lord iTunia & His iPods

Further down the path of this highway sat a new and more promising market where one might find the same joy that once was had in the presence of an unopened 7-inch. The prophet did settle into it and see its merits as a path of righteousness but was soon pissed at his friends' very inability to properly label their stupid ripped mp3s properly just one time! I mean how fucking hard is it to simply put a disc in the drive and WRITE DOWN all the info if you're gonna share the damned thing? What the hell is 01 Track 01 01 01_ _ .mp3? Some obscure Rush reference?

The Guitar Centurians

After his dismissal from the council of those stupid geeks and their clicky little P2P group on Planet Sensitive, the prophet did find himself at the steps of a blindingly lit edifice. Once inside, his eyes were treated to a feast of beautiful works of sonic majestry, and their prices were so reasonable as to mock their very makers, enslaved in far-off countries and fed little more than dirt and hair. He reached for one of these fine instruments to soothe his soul from the slough of despond he'd been figuratively cast into by those fucking nancies on that bitchy little bright-eyes forum. At once he was met with an intricately illustrated guitarist bejewelled by nostril, ear, and eyebrow. The guitarist had flames licking from the bottom of his flash robe and a pair of dice emblazoned on the breast. His nameplate read "Larry." His beard was knit into a small strand of rope. "Shall I play for you?" he asked. "If you can beat me at solo-off, I'll throw in a bag of picks and a PowerRammer 25 for only $10 on an already marked-down $675. This mama screams and creams, trust me."

The Bonacoachapaloozavans

In the age of the arena-rock concert, many became disenchanted with the idea of seeing what might be a famous band but might also be a speck of dung on an unwashed toilet seat perform half of the band's canon, badly and out of order. Lo, even the enormous TV screen projected what the specks of dung were doing on the distant stage was well nigh lame and not worth the $50 price of admission. Soon, acts of note began to play to fewer than five thousand people all sitting twenty-five seats away from one another and four hundred on the floor stoned and drunk and bored by the cheap light show. This unearthed the first great dragon, the Lollapaloot, and she was beheld as a beautiful creature, like her ancestor born of the summer of love, the Woodstach, as she held many possibilities and was cool and free and not nearly as big of a downer as her big sister, LiveAidathan. Several years did she live, roaming the country and parading her beauty for all to see at astonishing cost. She begat many offspring that would beckon the youthful with promises of visions, merriment, funnel cakes, and blonde bombshell lipstick lesbian hippie chicks that shave their pits, have group sex, and listen to radio alternarock instead of the doddering banjo witchcraft that actual hippies listen to. The Bonarroot and the Coachellavan were eventually plopped out of her vast pissflaps after getting pinned and mounted by the Horned Readingberry on a summer trip to England.

The Scrolling Rune

In an earlier time, the scrolls were handed down from elder to younger for guidance and knowledge. Their passages were great in length, their coverage vast and various, and their "best of" lists were annual. As time

went on, the scrolls became shorter and less varied, and their lists unnumbered such as to make an issue of the Chunkleteer appear to be straight prose. Indeed, not only did the scrolls begin to suck, but such was their place in rock history an institution and tantamount to rock law that ALL rock criticism was, by millennium's end, reduced to the likes of eighteen full-color double-truck pictures and only three paragraphs spread across six pages.

The XMTV Channel of Reality Rock Gameshow Concerts

And there the prophet sat at the very end of what could possibly be described as "Rock, bruh" and gazed into the abyss that was the Arockalpyse. The great podcast from SXCMJ3000's very own streaming HDvideo site XMTVChannel of Reality Rock Gameshow Concerts. As the moronic offspring of all of the worst ideas to break a band and somehow give it "buzz," a new "user-controlled" podcast-video contest that pits bands stupid enough to pay an arbitrary entry fee against videos uploaded from tivo dating no later than 1982 and no longer than 45 seconds.

DAG LUTHER GOOCH

The Saints & the Sinners

For so God had man for fodder with which to screw around; however, this pathetic, mortal creation is the inevitable social failure know as "the band." It is at such "bands" that this book is directed. Thus, we give thanks to the begotten who have forsaken our commandments and subsequently begat new ones. Here are some of the notable ill-gotten gains of our cosmic loins who have generously fed grist to our sanctified mill. May God have mercy on their souls.

The "5" Royales, The 101'ers, A Certain Ratio, Abba, AC/DC, Acid Mothers Temple, Bruce Adams, Hasil Adkins, Lou Adler, The Adolescents, The Adverts, Agent Orange, Steve Albini, GG Allin, Alternative TV, Angelic Upstarts, Angry Samoans, The Angry Samoans, Antiseen, The Apples (in Stereo), Archers of Loaf, Don Arden, Mark Arm, Art Ensemble of Chicago, Neil Aspinall, Chet Atkins, The Avengers, David Axelrod, Albert Ayler, The B-52's, Burt Bacharach, Bad Brains, Badfinger, Ed Bahlman, Lester Bangs, Syd Barrett, Bathory, Bauhaus, Jeff "Skunk" Baxter, The Beatles, Jorge Ben, Benjamin, Claude "Kickboy Face" Bessy, Jello Biafra, Big Boys, Big John, Big Star, Birthday Party, Black Flag, Black Randy and the Metrosquad, Black Sabbath, Art Blakey, Blowfly, Blue Cheer, Marc Bolan, John Bonham, Booker T. and the MG's, Sonic Boom, Boredoms, Boris, Born Against, David Bowie (up until '78), Joe Boyd, The Boys, John Brannon, Bread, James Brown, Lenny Bruce, Bill Bruford, Lindsey Buckingham, Jeff Buckley, Tim Buckley, R.L. Burnside, Buzzcocks, Cabaret Voltaire, John Cage, Cab Calloway, Can, Captain Beefheart, Captain Beyond, Carcass, Walter and Wendy Carlos, James Carr, Dylan Carson, Laura Carter, Mother Maybelle Carter, Neko Case, Johnny Cash, Nick Cave, Celtic Frost, James Chance, Art Chantry, Rhys Chatham, Cheap Trick, Leonard and Phil Chess, Chic, Billy Childish, Alex Chilton, Cheetah Chrome, Gene Clark, The Clash, The Clean, Cockney Rejects, Nik Cohn, Ornette Coleman, Mick Collins, Conflict Magazine, Ry Cooder, Julian Cope, Stewart Copeland, Elvis Costello, Count

Grishnackh, country music before and after '55, Cows, The Cramps, Crass, Dave Crider, Crime, Aleister Crowley, The Crucifucks, Chuck D., D.O.A., The Damned, Dangerhouse Records, Glenn Danzig, Davey Jones with the King Bees, Dead Boys, Dead Kennedys, Claude Debussy, Deep Purple, Devo, Dickies, Didjits, Ronnie James Dio, Dion, DJ Kool Herc, D.O.A., Dog Faced Hermans, Don Caballero, Lee Dorsey, Dow Jones and the Industrials, Tom Dowd, Dr. John, Nick Drake, Tomata du Plenty, Marcel Duchamp, Ian Dury, Bob Dylan, E.L.O., Steve Earle, Earth Wind and Fire, Eater, Einstürzende Neubauten, The Electric Eels, Elf Power, Brian Eno, Brian Epstein, Roky Erickson, ESG, Esquivel, Mal Evans, Yatmatsuka Eye, The Faces, Jad Fair, Marianne Faithful, Farina, Richard and Mimi, Fear, Feederz, The Feelies, Danny Fields, Larry "Wildman" Fischer, Flatt & Scruggs, Flipper, Brigitte Fontaine, Richmond Fontaine, Kim Fowley, The Free Design, Robert Fripp, Bill Frisell, Fugazi, The Fugs, Serge Gainsbourg, Galaxie 500, Gang of Four, The Gap Band, Marvin Gaye, Generation X, Genesis, Germs, João Gilberto, Greg Ginn, Michael Gira,

The Gizmos, Vic Goddard, Albert Goldman, Bill Graham, Rob Gretton, The Gun Club, Woody Guthrie, Lance Hahn, Hanatarash, Herbie Hancock, Kathleen Hanna, Hanoi Rocks, Grant Hart, Harvey Milk, Screamin' Jay Hawkins, Hawkwind, Tom Hazelmyer, Lee Hazelwood, Richard Hell, Helmet, Jimi Hendrix, Pierre Henry, heroin (the drug, not the band), Paul Hewson, Hipgnosis, Robyn Hitchcock, Barry Hogan, Buddy Holly, Peter Holsapple, Josh Homme, John Lee Hooker, Lightnin' Hopkins, Son House, Mike Hudson, Humble Pie, Mississippi John Hurt, Hüsker Dü, Iggy and The Stooges, Il Duce, Iron Maiden, The Jam, Jandek, Joan Jett, Penn Jillette, Jobriath, Robert Johnson, Daniel Johnston, John Paul Jones, Louis Jordan, Journey, Joy Division, Judas Priest, John Kalodner, Andy Kaufman, Sonny Kay, Nick Kent, Tim Kerr, Killing Joke, Lemmy Kilmister, King Crimson (pre-Adrian Belew & Tony Levin), Don Kirshner, Klaatu, Allen Klein, Kraftwerk, Fela Kuti, Kit Lambert, Leadbelly, Led Zeppelin, John Lennon, Ted Leo, Jerry Lee Lewis, Jerry Lewis, Liquid Liquid, Little Richard, Von Lmo, Alan Lomax, Lord Buckley, The Louvin

Brothers, Love, Lucifer (the entity, not the band), Lydia Lunch, Bascom Lamar Lunsford, John Lydon, Jeff Lyne, Loretta Lynn, Lynyrd Skynyrd, Shane MacGowan, Ian MacKaye, Uncle Dave Macon, Magazine, Jeff Mangum, Handsome Dick Manitoba, Johnny Marr, Sir George Martin, J Mascis, John Mayall, Curtis Mayfield, Mayhem, The MC$_5$, Alan McGee, Blind Willie McTell, MDC, Meat Puppets, The Meatmen, Joe Meek, Mekons, Melvins, Metal Urbain, The Meters, Minor Threat, Minutemen, Miracle Legion, Mission of Burma, Joni Mitchell, Mogwai, The Monks, Bill Monroe, Keith Moon, Slim Moon, Moondog, Ennio Morricone, Keith Morris, Morrissey, Mark Mothersbaugh, Mudhoney, Brendan Mullen, The Mummies, The Music Machine, My Bloody Valentine, Napalm Death, Nardwuar the Human Serviette, The Nation of Ulysses, Necros, Negative Approach, Fred Neil, Neon Boys, Michael Nesmith, Neu!, Neurosis, New Bomb Turks, New York Dolls, Nico, Harry Nilsson, Nirvana, Jack Nitzsche, Klaus Nomi, Laura Nyro, The O'Jays, The Obsessed, Phil Ochs, Andrew Loog Oldham, Pauline Oliveros, The Olivia Tremor Control, The Only Ones, Operation Ivy, Genesis P. Orridge, Os Mutantes, Ozzy Osbourne, Shuggie Otis, Wendy O'Williams, Ian Paice, Soo Young Park, Colonel Tom Parker, Gram Parsons, Charley Patton, Pavement, Neil Peart, David Peel, John Peel, Ralph Peer, Pere Ubu, Lee "Scratch" Perry, Oscar Peterson, P-Funk, John Phillips, Pink Floyd (pre-The Wall), The Pixies, Poison Idea, Robert Pollard, Peter Prescott, Billy Preston, Joe Preston, The Pretenders, Prince, Prince Paul, Richard Pryor, Punk Magazine, Pylon, Queen, Radio Birdman, Ramones, Ramrod, Otis Redding, Lou Reed, Steve Reich, Terry Reid, John Reis, The Replacements, Rezillos, Buddy Rich, The Rich Kids, Jonathan Richman, Terry Riley, Rites of Spring, Rocket From The Tombs, Jimmie Rodgers, Wayne Rogers, Pen Rollings, Henry Rollins, Dexter Romweber, The Ronnettes, Mick Ronson, Nino Rota, Roxy Music, Todd Rundgren, Rush, Corey Rusk, Jay Ryan, Greg Sage, Buffy Sainte-Marie, The Saints, Sky Saxon, Vin Scelsa, Lalo Schifrin, Bon Scott, Gil Scott-Heron, Sebadoh, Kevin Seconds, Tony Secunda, Pete Seeger, Sham 69, Greg Shaw, Kevin Shields, Shonen Knife, Gene

Simmons, Nina Simone, Simply Saucer, Siouxsie and the Banshees, Slash Magazine, Slayer, Sleep, The Slits, The Small Faces, Bessie Smith, Fred "Sonic" Smith, Harry Smith, Jimmy Smith, Mark E. Smith, Patti Smith, Soft Boys, The Soft Machine, Sonic Youth, The Sonics, Spacemen 3, Otis Spann, Sparks, Phil Spector, Skip Spence, Jon Spencer, Bruce Springsteen, Owsley Stanley, Gertrude Stein, Bill Stevenson, Jim Stewart, Stiff Little Fingers, Sly Stone, Joe Strummer, Poly Styrene, Subway Sect, Suicide, Sun Ra, Superchunk, Stu Sutcliffe, Swans, Swell Maps, Tar, Cecil Taylor, Television, Joe Tex, Thin Lizzy, This Heat, Dave Thomas, Richard Thompson, Chris Thomson, Big Mamma Thornton, Keith Matthew Thornton, Tiny Tim, The Troggs, Ike Turner, Jeff Tweedy, UK Subs, Uriah Heep, Van Halen, Don Van Vliet, Townes Van Zandt, The Velvet Underground, The Ventures, Void, Jon Von, Klaus Voorman, Porter Wagoner, Tom Waits, Scott Walker, Wall of Voodoo, Bill Ward, Muddy Waters, Doc Watson, Jimmy Webb, Ween, The Weirdos, Jann Wenner, Bob Weston, Bukka White, The Who, Whodini, Hank Williams, Brian Wilson, Dennis Wilson, Jackie Wilson, Robert Wilson, Tony Wilson, Wire, Howlin' Wolf, Stevie Wonder, Link Wray, Robert Wyatt, X, XTC, Yo La Tengo, Young Marble Giants, Neil Young, David Yow, Frank Zappa, Thalia Zedek, Zero Boys, Zombies and ZZ Top.

Thanks

Blessed be those whose involvement was diectly or indirectly helpful to the construction of this hallowed text. In no special order, we'd like to thank Mack's Lounge, Carlisle's (R.I.P. ya'll), Dean and Company (Deanie for bagpiping, Podo for sword fighting), the original Georgia Road, Tender's Herb and Spices, sodium benzoate, the day jobs, the Benedictine Hand, Foxy Target Practice and Nails, sex that is never on the beach, the Irondale Café, Dell's Den (we'll stay out of the parking lot from now on, Dell), Jasper John's "Target with Four Faces" screenplay, Tom "The Rock and Roll Travel Agent" Pisano, 14-inch teardrop hanging gazing balls, Edy's Grand Vanilla ice cream, jerk-chicken eating contests, Texas-style roadhouses in strip malls, Kate Jackson's original hair, *Toastmaster 2: The Musical*, Cheetah (my pillow), all ya'll whose last name rhymes with "Orange," sassy finger waving, Premium Washington Extra Fancy Braeburn Apples, Gregory Peccary, Lloyd at Imaginary Records, the Book of Acts and most of the Book of Dirty Acts, Tarrant, Alabama General Vulgarity the professional wrestler, Christopher Gluck, Terry Branson and the Ozark Mountain Boys, Buck and Chuck at Vinyl Solutions, Ovid, Inspectors #253 and #447, shows at Storkland's, ailment answers, full-moon mooning, 6-inch potted miniature roses, Reed Books, Coach Wood, bottle rockets shot in my parents' closet, the short-lived Four Foot Club, Sir Speedy, innovative solutions, Studio 21 Hair Salon (Henry *looooved* your tanning bed), Elbert Hubbard, handicapped driver services, Liberty Wishes the stripper, divorce lawyer Damon "DS" Smith, the ol' collegiate try, Norton's flowers, Tompson's Frame Factory, Cameron Soth Corp., "Workin' Magic," plumbing problems, Jubilee Joe's, population explosions, Seneca (we hardly knew you), razzle-dazzle and razz-ma-tazz, Tomlin Excavating and Demolition, dog guard guards, landscape nurserymen, Ed Cannon Roofing, Inc., Wags to Riches dog bone store, Bone Dali, jazz hands, Antonin Artaud's "Theatre of Cruelty," that guy who grunts numbers in Spanish at the Highland Athletic Club, Nipsey Russell, Bobby T, Miss Spain's fourth-grade class, the now defunct pets.com spokes-puppet, Smencil's Gourmet Scented Pencils (especially the fruit punch scent), the word "granular," my postman Jim, African bush baby gophers, Rufus "Tee Tot" Payne, pantyhose slingshots, Willie Nelson's Country Peach Cobbler ice cream, Avondale Cleaners, caller ID, Key Underwood Coon Dog Memorial Graveyard, Mama Petite, tiny bows and arrows made of paperclips and rubber bands, The Voluntary Human Extinction Movement, Harpoons 'R' Us, delicious dead things, Childless By Choice–brand frozen dinners, Wholesale Caskets, Bacon 'n' Badges, LLC, Ian and Jeff (as always), Cornish pasties, bobblehead dolls of players who have been traded, Vlad the Inhaler, macramé jockstraps, Feng Shui cemeteries, all ya'll indoorsy types, the Birmingham-Jefferson County Transit Authority, some (but not all) of my gonads, the stray hairs on the toilet seat, Kay-Lee (my baby girl) and her sister Shasta (from another daddy), Ol' "Blood ' n' Guts" Malone for being so patient, every drop of my Milky Way, our cow Delilah (for sharing), the Glory Hole Museum in the eighth dimension of my mind, Ms. Saipan's Full Release Parlor, the second coming, Yoga Girl, numbers 6 and 57 (we won again!), chloralmethohydrate, NASA, Bert (but not Ernie), the sound of children's laughter when someone breaks a hip, polysynthetic nonrecyclable paper, Cupcakez (my hamster), the two guys who invented "butt rivets," Chester A. Arthur, the 1964 New York Mets (thought you could get one past me, huh?), Uncle Floyd, Goriddle from the Great Space Coaster, the River Bottom Nightmare Band, Frank Zappa's beard, Dinty Moore's low-sodium beef stew, Red Hot Chili Peppers' "Stadium Arcadium" box set, BB King, the "buy one, get one free" scam, strip-mall corporate-chain barbecue restaurants, the iTunes store, Elaine Bryant, Fruit Roll Ups and/or edible underwear, Sharpie© (not the marker), Owens-King Insurance, The Paw-Paw Patch, St. John's of Mt. Laurel Episcopal Church, Mattel's motorized Courtney Love, my brightest cubic zirconia, fighting babies, your mama, alt-weekly music editors, Shelby County, Arkansas, my local Narrow Path of Righteousness book store, roast beef and provolone sandwiches, Eilert Lövbörg, the only wandering Jew in Grant Park (where are all ya'll?), all my dawgs that participated in this year's Iditarod, the Tommy Bartlet Water Extravaganza Hour half-time show, jazz hands, Red Jimmy's bathtubs, The Chick'n

Rub, Lord Tango's Ball Emporium, the male members of the Lorne Bushell family, Small, Medium, and Double-X, black folks who agree that Kwanzaa is stupid, the Snuggle fabric softener bear and his trademark giggle, Bhutan's claim as "The Happiest Country in the World," Grendel's Grundel, herpetologists, the National Do-Not-Call List, blood oranges, Epson "Big Nuts" Lavender, the Pawleys Island Posse, the Mongolian calendar, ethnic musics, the 50-yard bummer, Indian rope burns, the "good" cancer, "viral" videos, bicycle seat warmers, wild pitches during an intentional walk, midgets vs. dwarves, jalapeño-popper corn dogs, Rüüd Mortuary and Funeral Services, the likeness of Ulysses S. Grant, mint juleps everywhere, the ladies in red hats who meet for dinner, ants, aunts and Antz, saying "that's really funny" instead of laughing, self-locking freezer bags, factory car stereos, subtle nuances, the way we were, cock flattery, crock pots, fly swatter guns, slight deviations on the missionary position, that Hummer that is also a truck, recipes containing secret herbs and spices, Old Spice, dollar store loyalty, scoopable litter, powerful odor removers, super powers, double coupons, gettin' some, nick-names that are both mean and accurate, seeing that guy at the Carbondale Mall wearing an Exploited shirt and with eyeliner and that ridiculous bowlers cap, the mystery of redheads, islands, fjords, folding combs, blushing, allergy relief, getting "Shower Fresh" fresh, dogs and cats everywhere, a lack of truly haunted low-rent housing, revenge fantasies, old men who are pillars of impotent rage, those new nickels that I sometimes look at, critical race theorists, metaphors, Tab (the delicious one-calorie soft drink), sports, porn that tries to make a difference, gettin' all my props, flossing regularly, Christian Beard Lovers Association, The Bargain Carousel, inconsolably bad art shows, Just for Kicks Dance Studio, Caribbean Joe, Hay Fever by Noel Coward, Okie-Dokie 2-pc. Sets, haunted mansions, Ambrielle Smooth Revolution balcony push-up bra, the Moline Barons Bing-Bong Club, the El Paso quesadilla, the odontophore, Kicks 106, Hummel fetishists, campfire story "accidents," the Ypsilanti Huskers, Margot Kidder's mental breakdown, The Land of Women Chicken Shack, Stars and Stripes with Scrubbin' Bubbles, Alan Hineline's Twist performed by the Alabama Ballet, creative mammal classification, The

Woodentops, Green Valley Baptist, Southminster Saints, *The Cherry Orchard* by Anton Chekhov, Bahaism-lite, Telluride's downfall, Maw Maw and Paw Paw (they're still just cootin' around), Model VVP-48 portable phonograph with speakers that separate up to 20 feet the '78 Ford Bronco, Hungry Jack Big Tastin' Biscuits, Pineapple Spamloaf, the Cheddar Hot Dog Melt-Over, Heavenly Devilish Bacardi Rum Cakes, Unguentine aerosol first-aid for sunburn, Nerfoop, the giant Inflatable Giraffe Toss Set, Easy Riders by Roadmaster AMF, Hobie Skateboards, Billy the toy sheep, Outfit-Your-Dog-Like-Santa-Claus Kit, a boxful of smiles, people who refuse to say "preggers," Iron Mike Sharp, "Vowel Tooth" Jenkins, three of the five members of The Missing Gerbils, every professional wrestling manager, Esteban, reliable windshield wipers, anyone who has ever walked through a screen door, Derby Parkway, Diet Coca-Cola Plus, the Fisher-Price® Adventure People, the Panasonic Funnygraph, Video Beam Television, Tottenham Hotspur, the extras of Gigli, Nottingham Rock City, Jell-O gelatin apricot salad with chicken dinner, One Call Funeral, Cremation and Cemetery Services, Southern Firearm Appraisals, Latham's Hair Clinic, Oumi's African hair braiding, Honky Tonk piano, tweenagers, salad dodging, Ruslana's "Wild Dance," Freedom Foot, the Puka, panty nuts, Hang Teen T's and Shorts, Dem Ole Lazy Bones Rib Joynt, Alaska's flag, Baby D, the adagio tempo, poet laureate John Dryden, some prime numbers, Mount of Venus, Neo-Classicism in the "Brown" Round, Giant Inflatable Penis Inc., Varicosis Cosmetic Laser Center, Payola, baby!, Party Foul Fart Spray, Joseph Lister (props for kicking out the creation of antiseptics, bro), proctalgia fugax, I'm a Stranger Here Myself Tour Guides, the Feel-Good Factor, rag-tatty underwear, Everything But The Kitchen Sink Kitchen Sink Shop, Different as Chalk & Cheese Fine Cheeses, slight technical hitches, all the horny men of Qatar, Harpy the circus act, Crazy Bill's Fireworks, European atmosphere, Thumpers, Carnival Season, lap dances while sitting on futons, Bill Watson's beef trust, Aziz's stress incontinence, Super Balls Out Christmas Sweaters, John Varvatos (thanks for the custom suede jock strap), the Artie Bucco's line of dressing and sauces, Yippe-ki-yay, Motherfucka Crab Claw Dressing, Nigel Slater of Real Food, DVD Region 5, Lil and Jill at Coyote Ugly,

William MacReady, Festoon, Theater Curtains, Beulahland, Muckraker-brand rakes, Gynecomastia, The Discovery Place, the more burly Earl, Ollie's World Famous KKK BBQ wild geese that fly with the moon on their wings, The Reading Rainbow, Bartholin's Glands, Biore nose strips, Frisco-brand Speedballs, the Little Casino, ASFA goober kids, bib overalls, "Bubba Don't You Lose That Number" Karaoke Bar, Dr. Jeckles, Vacation Bible School, First Frost, seersucker suits, King Biscuit Blues, the way Athens used to be, the guide staff at the Cyclorama, Peyronie's Disease, Through Thick and Thin Cosmetic Surgery of the Penis Center, Ye-Call-Me-Old Fashion Senior Center, Blessing in Disguise Calamity Team, Reverend Howard Finster's Hallelujah Syrup, Hooters' poppers, Bing Bing Dust, The Cookie and Candyman, Uncle Emil's Sniff 'n' Snort, Jock Squad, Hippie Johnny, ghost-busting crack, gettin' "Cabbage-Face Eff'd Up," Tragic Magic, Bite-Off-More-Than-You-Can-Chew Steakhouse, belly button discharge, the old Auburn crew, Ganglion, hairiness in women, Corporate Hipsters (that have died), the cries of all lost children at the supermarket, 3:06 AM (the new 4:20, duh), black on black crime, fishy business, anal leakage of any kind, Noggin the Nog & Nogbad the Bad, upturned turtles of Galapagos Islands, Minor Treat (London's only DIY "fun-sized" hardcore chocolate shop), maiming the firstborn, talkin' bout your generation, fixins bars, Kum-N-Go gas stations, bartering, wordsmiths, Fisher's Man Wharf, Tom Raper's RV, Vaughn A. Wamsley personal injury attorney, headset mics, dates with Destiny, fava beans, putting some "serious stank" on it, animal husbandry, Thai One On massage parlor and tapas restaurant, the Meals-on-Seals program for terminally ill people on icebergs, LiquidMeat™, Pastrami Sport Drink, Zeke (no, *you* pass the ketchup!), Butterfingers Lamont (the only honest three-card-monty dealer on the East Coast), The Association for the Advancement of Cherries Other Than Bing, Filthy Bob, Riboflavin, Stinger Harris (the American flying ace who mistakenly shot down 30 German planes between 1985–88), The Stank, all our fond memories of Rod Stewart passing out and having his stomach pumped, seemerot.com, my coffee slingin' n-words at Aurora Coffee.

List of Contributors

Original Concept
Brian Teasley and Henry H. Owings

Editors & Proofreaders
Iain Hinchcliffe, Benn Ray, Jeff McLeod, Patrick Gough, Emerson Dameron, Randy Haward

Major Contributors
Tom Bagby, Billy Carter, Emerson Dameron, Andrew Earles, Dag Luther Gooch, Patrick Gough, Neil Jendon, Tony King, Jeff McLeod, Benn Ray, Eric Rovie, Scott Sosebee, Brian Teasley

Other Contributors
Kristin Amarante, David Andler, Greg Araya, Michael Babcock, Allison Baker, Ana Balka, Dave Barbe, Tony Bennett, Steve Birmingham, Nick Blakey, John Branon, Don Breithaupt, Jonny Browning, Syd Butler, Jesse Capps, David Carr, Nadine Cheung, Armando Celentano, Mike Cooley, Scott Cox-Stanton, Dale Crover, John Cummings, Craig Curtice, Daylen Dalrymple, John Darnielle, Thomas Davies, Ben Davis, John DeCicco, Rob Del Bueno, Jason Dove, Kevin Duneman, Mark Duston, Marah Eakin, Michael Faloon, Gary Flom, Michael T. Fournier, Adam Goren, Andres Galdames, Garland Gallaspy, Larry Getlen, Ben Gibbard, Jacob Glenn-Levin, Ben Goldberg, Joseph Grey, Mike Grimes, Jason Groth, Myk Guanci, Meseret Haddis, Dan Hadley, Cash Hartzell, Randy Harward, Paul Heiger, Karl Heitmueller, Ben Hellman, Andrea Herman, Shane Hickey, David Hickox, Iain Hinchliffe, Douglas Holland, Patterson Hood, David Hood, Marc Horton, Sean Howe, Oliver Hunt, Mathis Hunter, Leah Hutchinson, John Iskander, Chris Jacobs, Nicholas Jaster, Garth Johnson, Joseph Kelly, Dryw Keltz, Ever Kipp, Tad Kubler, Gordon Lamb, Ted Leo, Ballard Lesemann, Daniel Littlewood, Dan London, Joe Loverde, Brendon Lloyd, Joe Macleod, Andy Maddox, Charles Maggio, Neil Mahoney, Jordan Mamone, Bob Marshall, Mike McGonigal, Liam McKaharay, Kyle McKinnon, Eugene Mirman, Chris Mooney, Cash V. Morris, Anthony Moschella, Steve Myers, Alex Naidus, Ayal Naor, Ashley Nix

Fucich, Les Nuby, Adam Oliansky, Patton Oswalt, Sarah Weston Hayes Owings, Ed Parker, T.S. Pearson, Rob Andrist Plourde, Joe Plummer, Brian Pluta, Talmadge Price, Melanie Redmond-Guanci, Drew Reiter, Albert Ricci, Luther Rochester, Henry Rollins, Jim Romeo, Dave Schools, Pete Schreiner, Robert Schriner, Mahmood Shaikh, Kip Shepherd, Eryc Donovan S., Millicent Souris, Kyle Spence, Matthew Taylor, Jack Teague, Sean Tejaratchi, Larry Tenner, Matthew Traxler, Willy Tyler, Brian Turner, Josh Vanek, Dr. Jonathan Waks, Mark Wasserman, Terrence White, Dean Whitmore, Brian Whitney, Pete Wilkins, Davin Wood, Kaya Yamashita, and the many faceless contributors from the comments section on the chunklet.com site.